STRUCTURED GROUPS FOR FACILITATING DEVELOPMENT

New Vistas in Counseling Series
Series Editors—Garry Walz and Libby Benjamin
In collaboration with ERIC Counseling and Personnel Services Information Center

Structured Groups for Facilitating Development: Acquiring Life Skills, Resolving Life Themes, and Making Life Transitions, Volume 1
Drum, D. J., Ph.D. and Knott, J. E., Ph.D.

New Methods for Delivering Human Services, Volume 2
Jones, G. B., Ph.D., Dayton, C., Ph.D. and Gelatt, H. B., Ph.D.

Systems Change Strategies in Educational Settings, Volume 3
Arends, R. I., Ph.D. and Arends, J. H., Ph.D.

Counseling Older Persons: Careers, Retirement, Dying, Volume 4
Sinick, D., Ph.D.

Parent Education and Elementary Counseling, Volume 5
Lamb, J. and Lamb, W., Ph.D.

Counseling in Correctional Environments, Volume 6
Bennett, L. A., Ph.D., Rosenbaum, T. S., Ph.D. and McCullough, W. R., Ph.D.

Transcultural Counseling: Needs, Programs and Techniques, Volume 7
Walz, G., Ph.D., Benjamin, L., Ph.D., et al.

Career Resource Centers, Volume 8
Meerbach, J., Ph.D.

Behavior Modification Handbook for Helping Professionals, Volume 9
Mehrabian, A., Ph.D.

STRUCTURED GROUPS FOR FACILITATING DEVELOPMENT

Acquiring Life Skills, Resolving Life Themes, and Making Life Transitions

David J. Drum
J. Eugene Knott

Vol. I in the New Vistas in Counseling Series
Series Editors—Garry Walz and Libby Benjamin

HUMAN SCIENCES PRESS
Formerly *BEHAVIORAL PUBLICATIONS INC.*
72 FIFTH AVENUE, NEW YORK, N.Y. 10011

Library of Congress Catalog Number 77-1947
ISBN: 0-87705-308-1

Copyright © 1977 Human Sciences Press
72 Fifth Avenue, New York, N.Y. 10011

Printed in the United States of America
789   987654321

Library of Congress Cataloging in Publication Data

Drum, David J
  Structured groups for facilitating development.

  (New vistas in counseling; v. 1)
  Bibliography: p.
  .ncludes index.
  1. Group psychotherapy.   I. Knott, J. Eugene, joint
author.   II. Title.   III. Series.
RC488.D76   616.8'915   77-1947
ISBN 0-87705-308-1

TABLE OF CONTENTS

FOREWORD

It all started with a phone call. We knew that a lot of new things were being done in group work—so new that they weren't even in ERIC yet. And our professional friends, knowing that we were involved in the business of pulling together disparate informational facets into one glittering gem, had asked if we couldn't provide them with a succinct targeted "package" that would update their knowledge and suggest new formats and approaches for their group efforts. So we called the person who we knew was right on top of what was happening—who not only was aware of what others were doing but was himself successfully creating and experimenting with innovative group techniques —Dave Drum. In a rather lengthy telephone discussion, he and we became excited about a possible publication, and before long we were down to the nuts and bolts of a contract. This volume is the result.

Together with his co-worker, Gene Knott, Dave has assembled some programs and practices that are right on the forefront of what's new in group work. Designed for experienced group leaders, this volume provides a wealth of background information about the structured developmental group movement, as well as specificity regarding program content. Just examine the Table of Contents and you will see that the authors cover the gamut of developmental structured groups—life skills, life themes, and life transition—and that they also include research concerning the emergence of these groups and evaluation of their effectiveness.

We believe that the authors really came through—that their monograph is all we had envisioned, and more. They have tapped the expertise of others and included programs developed under their own aegis, and the result is a comprehensive compilation of "now" groups.

We do emphasize that this publication is not for everyone—the novice group leader may find that the "structure" is not structured enough and may want to acquire more skill in group process before tackling what is described here. But experienced group leaders hopefully will find that this publication whets the appetite and starts them on a gourmet search for the latest and finest fare in group work.

We think you will find this publication to be substantive and informative and hope you will agree that it should be required reading for all persons working to facilitate the development of individuals through the group approach.

Garry R. Walz and Libby Benjamin
Director and Associate Director, ERIC/CAPS

ACKNOWLEDGMENT

We wish to express our gratitude to all the talented people who have willingly shared the structured group programs they have devised. This book could not have been written without their essential contributions. Also, we are grateful to Libby Benjamin for her editorial support and suggestions throughout the realization of the manuscript, and to Al Southworth for his most useful critical comments. Special thanks, too, go to Jo-Ann Lepore and Linda McGowan for their patient perseverance in typing numerous drafts of the materials in this book.

Chapter 1

ORIGIN OF STRUCTURED GROUPS

The purpose of this book is to provide an overview of a relatively new style of helping people that can facilitate their growth and development. Within the past five years, a substantial number of highly structured group programs aimed at teaching key skills or clarifying important life attributes has been devised. Interest in utilizing structured group approaches is rapidly expanding, and has reached the point where a national Clearinghouse for Structured Group Programs has been established at the University of Rhode Island. These structured group approaches supply both effective learning strategies and interpersonal environments in which people can seek to achieve higher levels of personal competence and nurture feelings of inner satisfaction with the direction of their lives.

Structured groups are not to be viewed merely as a contemporary extension of the human-potential movement, although some roots may be perceived therein. Rather, these approaches should be viewed as educational tools whose implementation at the appropriate point in the evolution of an individual's development can facilitate positive growth. This work attempts to demonstrate the degree to which the structured group movement has matured and enhanced the capacity for practitioners to help people resolve both existing problems and developmental needs. To achieve this goal, the book provides an overview of the theoretical basis for structured groups and the critical elements in their design. Following that, three major categories of structured groups, their core components, and models for their development and implementation are described. Subsequent chapters present specific examples of each of the three major types of groups, their formats, and characteristics. Finally, the book addresses the issue of deployment of resources in utilizing such approaches to serve one's clientele, and the future needs of and directions for employing structured developmental groups.

DEFINITION OF STRUCTURED GROUPS

A structured group is a delimited learning situation with a predetermined goal, and a plan designed to enable each group member to reach this identified goal with minimum frustration and maximum ability to transfer the new learning to a wide range of life events. The use of structure in counseling groups allows the group facilitator: (1) to focus precisely on a specific goal and include relevant goal-oriented activities while eliminating goal-detracting influences; (2) to converge resources and exercises in order to amplify learning; and (3) to assess the degree of goal accomplishment for each participant. These three primary values of structuring, plus some other features, are highlighted by Middleman and Goldberg (1972) in their article on "The Concept of Structure in Experiential Learning."

They state:

> A structured learning situation is a closed system deliber-
> ately constructed and set in motion by the trainer or facilita-
> tor. It has a boundary which separates it from the talk about
> the situation as well. . . . Within this boundary a set of condi-
> tions is established which affects the roles and/or rules,
> and/or the processes of interaction. Finally, the trainer or
> facilitator introduces a task to be pursued under the struc-
> tured conditions. This task constitutes the moving dynamics
> of the learning situation. Participants must function within
> those particular conditions and experience both the oppor-
> tunities for and constraints on pursuit of the task and human
> behavior in general that are generated by these conditions.
> (p. 205)

For the purpose of clarifying the theoretical basis and
differentiating the goals of structured groups, they may be
categorized into three basic types: (1) those aimed at helping individuals acquire important interpersonal life skills;
(2) those directed toward enabling people to resolve and
understand critical life themes; and (3) those designed to
assist people in the making and completion of important
life transitions. Each of these three categories of structured
groups is the topic of a later chapter in this work.

THEORETICAL BASIS OF STRUCTURED GROUPS

The emergence of the structured group model is grounded
in several broader movements that have been gaining
momentum with the helping services professions. These
movements have been variously identified as affective education (Leonard, 1968; Borton, 1970; Brown, 1971; Purves,
1972; Castillo, 1974), psychological education (Alschuler,
1973; Guerney et al. 1970; Mosher and Sprinthall, 1971;
Ivey and Alschuler, 1973), humanistic education (Bessell &

Palomares, 1970; Weinstein & Fantini, 1970; Heath, 1971; Zahorik and Brubaker, 1972; Greer and Rubinstein, 1972; Patterson, 1973; Sharp, 1971), personal education and self-management (Bandura & Perloff, 1967; Watson and Tharp, 1972; Cudney, 1975; Thoreson & Mahoney, 1974; Williams & Long, 1975; Colley, 1975), or behavior modification (Goldiamond, 1965; Bandura, 1969; Lazarus, 1971).

Structured groups represent a convergence of many of these rather divergent helping styles, with each approach contributing some important elements both to the theory and design of a particular group. A common element apparent in almost all of these approaches is the emphasis placed on the educational–experiential format for overcoming difficulties or producing growth, rather than the more traditional one-to-one verbal process method of helping.

While the broad theoretical basis for structured groups is grounded in the approaches just identified, the specific goal of such groups is facilitating the developmental process and increasing the individual's adaptability to common life stresses. All too often the growth and development of the individual and his/her ability to handle life traumas have been left to chance resolution. In our own lives and the lives of people who surround us, one may find numerous examples of the unnecessary, nonproductive turmoil that occurs because no one offered assistance when individuals were at developmental crossroads or undergoing some traumatic transformation.

FACILITATING DEVELOPMENT

In order to achieve the goal of facilitating the developmental process, structured groups are often designed specifically to resolve a particular developmental task, such as learning to be an effective parent, being able to control anxiety, and/or gaining skill in setting realistic career and life goals. The study of the developmental tasks that confront individuals in the course of their lifetime is a relatively recent phenomenon. Only since the late 1930s has there been any systematic study of the various living and learning tasks of development an individual undergoes at various stages in life. But the impact of this way of viewing the needs of people has been mighty. Recognition—both of patterns of developmental needs and individual variability —has spurred numerous studies and writings, including those by Tryon and Lilienthal (1950), Havighurst (1953), Piaget (1954), Zaccaria (1965), Erikson (1968), Kohlberg (1970), Loevinger (1970), Perry (1970). In their formulation of the developmental process, these theorists frequently link identifiable growth periods to specific arrays of developmental tasks or outcomes. As a result of the identification of some predictable, regularly occurring life needs and growth tasks, it is becoming possible to anticipate their emergence and provide for early intervention.

Structured groups represent one important intervention useful in resolving critical developmental tasks when they first arise. Perhaps the most compelling value of the early intervention capability of structured groups is that, by enabling persons to resolve or fulfill a developmental task, they can prevent normal growth needs from deteriorating and becoming the basis for future life problems. The failure to accomplish adequately an earlier developmental task has been shown time and again to compound the difficulty in fulfilling subsequent needs and tasks in the developmental process. Guardo (1975), in an article on developmental existentialism, clearly illustrates the effect of unresolved problems on normal development in the following example:

> Let us use, as an illustration, a young woman whose father deserted her. If she cites this experience as a reason for her

inability to sustain a relationship with a young man, for fear
of being deserted again, then the helper must address two
issues: the residual psychological effects of the client's experience of desertion and the client's present inability to
sustain a heterosexual relationship. The helper should address these issues in their respective temporal contexts and
give attention to the progression of interpersonal development that the client has undergone between these times. . . .
If the young woman in the above illustration were twenty
years old, her situation would be interpreted quite differently from the way it would be if she were twenty-eight, since
the developmental expectations for interpersonal maturity
vary widely for these ages. (pp. 494–495)

Deteriorated life situations often presage full-blown
developmental crises. A client experiences futility when
he/she finds himself/herself immersed in a situational crisis without the wherewithal, because of earlier developmental deficits, to convert the challenge to a satisfactory,
growth-producing outcome. The relationship between unresolved developmental needs and the all-consuming vexa-
tion experienced in common situational crises is of major
consequence. The obvious counseling goal at that point is
to assist the individual to find the solution to the crisis. The
not-so-obvious secondary goal should be to help the individual learn a response style that will better serve him/her
in later attempts to avert such a crisis. The structured developmental group has built into it just such a dual capability. Application of this type of therapeutic strategy thus
simultaneously becomes both problem solving and preven-
tive, and possesses both short- and long-term benefits.

Some other elements in the dynamics of personal development deserve attention. First among these is the di-
chotomous nature of human development. Just as the
nature–nurture paradigm suffuses the whole of the behavioral sciences, so does this duality affect our notions of
which developmental tasks antecede others. The potentiality for most, if not all psychological development, is laid

down in the hereditary package one receives via genetic transmission. However, whether this potentiality is ever realized or actualized for a particular person is a function of the learning experiences encountered in the environment. And each of the developmental "gains" resulting from the successful integration of earlier learning becomes a prerequisite in the sequence of tasks necessary for the achievement of further personal competence. Thus, frustration of an early developmental task cannot help but thwart a related future developmental task.

Another interesting facet of the human developmental process is that in terms of both physical and social growth, the time wherein physiological development levels off occurs in close conjunction with the increasing need for expanded affective and interpersonal capabilities. It is also at this time that the individual is faced with the first major set of life "choices", particularly in this culture. Not coincidentally, this is the "site" of the largest number of structured developmental groups that have been developed to date. Even though late adolescence and early adulthood represent the focus of most structured group efforts, these groups often address developmental issues which originate from earlier, unfulfilled developmental needs.

The contemporary fact of life, documented so powerfully by Toffler (1970), which might be referred to as the "constancy of change," provides some indication of why the developmental period known as "adulthood" also represents an area of increasing response to structured groups. Contrary to the earliest theories of developmental psychology, recent studies have documented ongoing changes that pose developmental challenges for persons at midlife and later (Gould, 1972; Levinson et al., 1974; Poland, 1974; Lidz, 1976; Sheehy, 1976). The fact that "change" is an ongoing phenomenon and is occurring at an accelerating pace, demands that individuals acquire certain coping skills and adaptational abilities earlier and exercise them longer than was the case in previous generations, particularly in Western civilization. In many ways, the ultimate barometer of one's personal competence and self-actualization today is his/her capacity for coping with that "constancy of change."

INCREASING ADAPTABILITY TO STRESS

As we have increased our knowledge about the developmental process, we have also become increasingly aware of the deleterious effects that stress has on that process (Lazarus, 1966; Adams & Goldstein, 1970). When stressful circumstances exceed an individual's point of tolerance, his/her whole developmental thrust grinds to a halt. If a person's developmental history is riddled with unresolved needs, then he/she is further vulnerable to the crippling effects of extreme stress.

Most structured groups have the capacity to facilitate the process for working through deeply stressful feelings and at the same time to aid in the development of adaptive skills. Therefore, a woman who is in psychological transition—struggling with stressful feelings because, for example, she chooses to be more than a "shadow figure"—can be helped to resolve that stress. At the same time she can be exploring and developing alternative coping skills for enjoying her new style of being. Life transition groups are often designed both for resolving an existing problem and preparing for successful living in a different psychological (and sometimes physical) environment.

WHY STRUCTURED GROUPS?

The question of why should we invest time, energy, and resources in the development of structured groups instead of in the provision of traditional services can be viewed from several perspectives. First of all, structured groups enable the helping agent to time interventions to correspond as closely as possible to the origin of the developmental need. A serious limitation of traditional methods is that they are unable to provide intervention until long after an unmet developmental need has deteriorated into a deeply troubling problem.

The value of structured group approaches is not limited to the single dimension of timing. They also have several additional positive features for the practitioner and consumer.

Structured groups optimize time for the practitioner. Where particular developmental lags or needs can be diagnosed or anticipated, short-term learning-oriented group experiences can capitalize on what will always be insufficient counseling resources by focusing on specific behavioral components that form the core of the identified need. Offering such learning opportunities in a group format also has the advantage of addressing the similar needs of several people simultaneously. Building on already extant skills to update and vary counseling methodology, they offer a role change to the helping agent that is more in line with that of other "educators" and epitomizes the proactive stance. Furthermore, the built-in accountability dimension arising from the goal-oriented nature of the groups has tremendous importance, especially in current times of limited staff and finances.

Added gains accrue to consumers from a service modality that reaches out to them, often in their own living–working situation, and is time limited and target specific. An additional advantage for consumers is the benefit they realize from learning "responsiveness" ("intentionality," in psychological education terminology) to life situations as opposed merely to learning a discrete response to a specific situation.

SUMMARY

The introduction to this book has touched on the basic nature and genesis of structured groups for facilitating human development, some of the key elements in the process of development, and many of the characteristics that recommend such approaches both to the practitioner and the consumer. The next chapter describes the value of utilizing structured groups to help people deal with problem situations, the three major categories of structured groups, the core components of each of the three types, as well as a checklist for identifying and detailing the critical elements to be included in the development of a structured group.

Chapter 2

CONCEPTUAL OVERVIEW OF STRUCTURED GROUPS

VALUE OF STRUCTURED GROUPS

In general, structured groups represent attempts on the part of mental health workers to intervene as early as possible in an individual's life so that unmet normal developmental needs do not become the foundation for more serious problems later in life. Specifically, they are designed to provide opportunity for positive intervention to occur as the need for assistance develops. Thus, for example, instead of trying to help a person relieve his depression after an unsuccessful marriage, the focus is on intervening earlier to help a person learn how to communicate feelings nondefensively and how to share intimately. This illustration is characteristic of a number of situations in life where structured groups can reduce the likelihood that normal developmental needs will become frustrated and lead to the need for later extensive counseling and therapy.

Besides providing opportunity for early intervention, structured groups have several other positive attributes that make them valuable additions to the mental health worker's repertoire for promoting growth and development. Among the most important are the following:

1.   They demystify the process of self-discovery and self-enhancement by systematic structuring for goal attainment. Because the groups have a definite structure, they communicate a sense of goal-directedness and raise expectations that the goal can be achieved.

2.   They are relatively nonthreatening to participants and make the process of learning enjoyable. Through appropriate structured exercises they encourage people gently but firmly to increase their ability to try out new behaviors or examine issues they would normally avoid. Most structured groups attempt to raise a person's approach gradient so that he/she will attempt new behaviors or examine delicate issues, while traditional therapy focuses on lowering the avoidance gradient so that new behaviors may emerge.

3.   They allow for both peer and professional feedback relating to a specific interpersonal skill or life issue. Provisions are made for an individual to test reality, gain consensus, and explore self-enslaving myths. Peer involvement within the group in providing social feedback is a key factor in enabling participants to attempt new and provisional ways of responding to existing problem situations.

4.   They represent an economical use of treatment time. A significant number of issues or needs that are treated in one-to-one counseling can be more efficiently and completely resolved through a structured group.

5.   They encourage change and growth by providing a mechanism of active problem solving. Group members invest a significant amount of group time in practicing a

particular skill, actively clarifying an issue, and structuring a resolution.

6. They help participants become aware of the frequent occurrence of the type of problem situation they are attempting to resolve. The sense of "being in it together" is not only communicated through the fact that there are ten, twenty, or more participants in the particular group at hand but also that the type of group in which they are involved is being offered on a widespread basis in other locations.

7. They reduce the stigma associated with seeking help because they focus on common developmental needs utilizing an educational–experiential format. This is in contrast to traditional counseling that is largely remedial or rehabilitative in character.

8. They establish the boundaries of the contract between the leader and the participants and thereby create a sense of psychological safety for group members. Each participant can enter into the group experience with a feeling of inner comfort that the group will stick to the stated goal and not attempt to restructure the "whole personality." Many people fear that structured groups are simply sensitivity groups by another name and that their every vulnerability will be exposed and exploited. Through an explanation of the differences between the two types of groups, their fears can easily be relieved. The use of structure in groups sets real limits on the power of the leader and on what is legitimate to explore.

MAJOR TYPES OF STRUCTURED GROUPS

Structured groups can be classified into three general types, according to the emphasis the group leader and members place on achieving a specific purpose or goal. The three types are: (1) life skills groups, (2) life theme groups, and (3) life transition groups. While all these three types have an educational–experiential based format, are goal oriented, and utilize a systematic, sequential approach to the resolution of a problem situation, significant differences exist among them with regard to their goals. Broadly speaking, life skills groups are designed to help people acquire new skills or complete the development of inadequate skills. Life theme groups center on structuring the self-inquiry process so that an individual can develop a sense of personal understanding that can lead to greater feelings of freedom and individuation. Life transition groups have the twin goals of helping people psychologically restructure the past and enabling adaptation to an altered lifestyle. As one can see, each type of group aims at supporting and facilitating the developmental process from a different, yet often complementary, perspective.

Life Skills Groups

Life skills groups have as their common purpose helping people acquire or further develop life-enhancing skills that will enable them to cope successfully with the psychological demands of living. As a person's chronological age increases, especially during the first 18 to 25 years of life, the number of affective and interpersonal skills that must be mastered expands dramatically. Yet, although an individual is expected to develop this wide range of interpersonal skills, their acquisition is often left to chance. In today's society very few ceremonies, programs, or initiation rites remain that will insure the learning of critical life-enhancing skills by a given age (Aries, 1975). Despite this fact, we often show very little tolerance or provide little support for those people who have not learned certain skills by the expected time. The failure to acquire effective interpersonal skills impacts in a decidedly negative fashion on the quality of an individual's life.

Structured life skills groups provide procedures, methods, and systematic techniques to help people develop the affective and interpersonal skills they need to make life worth living. Some of the more common life skills workshops and groups are: Assertive Training, Anxiety Management, Career Planning, Behavioral Self-Control, Decision-Making/Problem-Solving, Communication Skills, Interpersonal Skills Training, and Parenting Skills.

CORE ELEMENTS.   Certain core elements are consistently stressed in life skills groups. First, in a life skills group the goal is always explicitly stated and is the reason for the group's existence. The leader provides for every participant a clear overview of the purpose of the group and the general methods that will be used to achieve that goal. It is critically important that the stated goal always remain the central focus for each group member. Second, life skills groups try to teach responsiveness to situations rather than merely discrete responses. A major goal of each group is to help people develop skill in responding or initiating as opposed to learning pat phrases or stock answers. Third, the typical format for a life skills group involves (a) a blending of didactic and experiential learning; (b) sequential and cumulative building from session to session; (c) out-of-group assignments to reinforce learning and increase generalization to real life; and (d) a predetermined number of sessions to achieve the stated goal. Fourth, virtually all life skills groups involve some preselection of clients. Specific selection criteria are established prior to the group that are based on the needs of the individual in relation to the group and the possible negative effects an individual may have on the group process. Fifth, life skills groups require that an atmosphere of mutual trust and cohesiveness exist among the members of the group. Because a large majority of the life skills groups utilize peer feedback as a reality—testing mechanism, it is important that life skills groups be time limited. The typical length of a group is usually between four and eight sessions and involves a total time commitment of 8 to 16 hours in formal meetings.

LEADER BEHAVIORS AND SKILLS.   Most often the leader takes a very active role during the life of the group by modeling appropriate behavior, role playing difficult or perplexing problems, providing positive reinforcement or constructive criticism, and assigning and reviewing homework. Thus, in order to be an effective facilitator of a life skills group, an individual must be able to communicate clearly, confront constructively, reinforce effectively, focus critical feedback to the task at hand, and understand the complexities of group process. In addition, the group leader must (1) be willing to adhere to the established goal and avoid turning the group into a nonspecific counseling group; (2) have command of a flexible fund of techniques and activities in order to vary the procedures or style used in attaining the goal when group conditions so indicate; (3) be comfortable with a leadership role limited to assisting with the accomplishment of a particular goal and the consequent reduction in power over the group; and (4) be willing to invest as much time and energy in designing and evaluating a particular type of group as in leading the actual group meetings. Since most life skills groups build from a theoretical base that is largely either behavioral or cognitive a working knowledge of relevant theories and research findings is also helpful.

While it is not essential for a prospective leader of structured groups actually to have developed the program to be offered, it is desirable that the person have had some experience as either a coleader or apprentice before becoming the primary leader. Apprenticing or cofacilitating allows the future group leader to obtain "hands-on" experience that will enable him/her to develop flexibility and avoid total dependence on the original design. Also, co-leading provides an opportunity to "clinic" group progress and, therefore, become sensitive to the critical points in the group movement. The majority of structured life skills groups are best cofacilitated.

Life Theme Groups

Contrasting with the life skills groups, that focus on skills necessary for positive interpersonal functioning, are the life theme groups. These groups are designed to provide individuals with opportunities to examine and grapple systematically with important intrapersonal issues of day-to-day living. Beginning with the period of adolescence, a substantial increase occurs in the number of times an individual is required to make subjective choices (Gould, 1972). Often external guidelines for choosing one alternative over another are unclear or conflict, and the person must look inward to determine which alternative is most appropriate. In short, the individual is forced to become his/her own resource for problem solving, making judgments, and evaluating alternatives, often with little preparation.

The choices an individual makes or the way he/she decides to exercise judgment are highly influenced by the extent to which the person has successfully resolved certain key life themes. For example, the degree to which a person has resolved his/her feelings about sexuality, personal values, mortality, and desire for intimacy clearly influence the way he/she will respond to others and to the environment. Most people can recall instances in their own lives or in the lives of acquaintances who have been so preoccupied with a particular issue or theme (mortality, loneliness, etc.) that all else became of little importance. Many people move through life unaware of how they affect other people and/

or how their ability to live in the "here and now" has become severely constricted because they have been unable to resolve some critical life theme.

One does not have to search very far to find situations where people have betrayed values central to themselves to escape feelings of loneliness or have chosen to live with surface-level relationships because real intimacy or sharing themselves with others was too difficult. Examples abound of how individuals have redirected their lives to compensate for inadequate resolution of central life issues. Life theme groups provide people with an opportunity to (1) examine their basic beliefs and values; (2) understand their style of relating to themselves; and (3) clarify the reasons why they related to others in specific ways. The ultimate goal of life theme groups is not simply to examine, understand, or clarify key life themes but to lead toward a resolution of those themes so that individuals can unshackle themselves from the constraints of an unexamined life and redirect themselves in more personally rewarding ways.

Just as the acquisition of many life skills is left to chance factors, so the resolution of important life themes is often left unprovided for in any systematic fashion. The advent of structured life theme groups offers a vehicle for systematic examination, evaluation, and resolution of important values, issues, or needs. Some examples of life theme groups or workshops are: Values Clarification, Male/Female Consciousness Raising, Meaning of Death in Life, Intimacy and Sharing, Loneliness and Self-Betrayal, Creating a Personal Lifestyle, Self-Esteem, and Learning to Love.

CORE ELEMENTS.   Life theme groups share a number of common characteristics. First, each life theme group has a clear purpose that is known to all group members and is the stated reason for the group's existence. Second, life theme groups focus on intrapersonal knowledge as opposed to the acquisition of interpersonal skills. The typical flow of the self-discovery process in a life theme group is exploration, integration, and initiation of the process of resolution. Third, through enabling people to increase their level of self-understanding, life theme groups help them become flexibly responsive to the needs and values of others rather than rigid or role dependent. Fourth, the group format typically involves (a) a series of structured exercises designed to direct and guide the self-inquiry process; (b) exercises or techniques for integrating and beginning resolution of life issues; (c) opportunity for processing feelings and attitudes uncovered as a result of the group activities; and (d) some guidelines indicating for whom the group is appropriate and whether a screening interview should be conducted. Fifth, life theme groups are value oriented in that they attempt to assist people to clarify their personal stance with regard to a specific theme or value. Finally, they are time limited. The typical group length varies from one to six sessions, with a corresponding investment of total time ranging from three to fifteen hours. Most life theme groups require a time investment for members of ten to twelve hours. Some life theme groups, however, are designed to be conducted in one day or one evening and, therefore, may last for as few as three hours.

LEADER BEHAVIORS AND SKILLS.   Even though life theme groups are highly structured, they often possess humanistic or existential foundations. The group leader plays an active, guiding role but is usually less active than the leader of a life skills group. The group leader must clearly explain each exercise, provide a system for processing new information or awareness, and seek to develop mutual trust and cohesiveness. In addition, much as in life skills groups, the leader of a theme group must (1) keep the group focus on the original goal; (2) have command of a flexible fund of techniques and activities so that he/she can redirect the style of goal attainment if group conditions so indicate; and (3) be willing to invest as much time and energy in designing and evaluating a particular type of group as in leading the actual group meetings.

Again, as in life skills groups, it is not essential for a prospective leader of structured groups actually to have developed the program to be offered, but it is desirable that the person have had some experience as either a coleader or apprentice before becoming the primary leader.

Life Transition Groups

Life transition groups are designed to help people understand, evaluate, and accomplish major changes which they feel are necessary or desirable. They attempt to help people move as smoothly and effectively as possible through the unexpected upheavals that occur in life as well as the conscious, willful attempts to undergo change.

People are constantly attempting to redirect or positively influence the course of their lives. One often hears statements like, "He is trying to better himself," "She's trying to be more sensitive," or, "He's trying to adjust to the kids' being gone." Many of the changes or transitions people experience are minor and can be accomplished without significant stress or fear of unknown consequences. However, when a person comes to the point of being suddenly catapulted into a new life style (death of a life mate, divorce, or other major upheaval), or purposefully seeks to alter an unfulfilling style of existence, he/she faces a very difficult and sometimes overwhelming challenge. Often the individual faces that task alone, unable to find helpful and supportive signposts. The feelings of apprehension, "second thoughts," and other negatively tinged emotions that sweep through a person entering a major life transition are magnified by the uncertainty of how to proceed or to comprehend what is happening.

In order to negotiate important life transitions successfully, an individual can profit from the assistance of an external resource system. The system should provide for a chance to test reality, find support for, and become aware of how others deal with change. Adopting a new way of life and adapting to it requires a high degree of intrapersonal awareness and a substantial array of interpersonal skills. Moving from a previous way of being to a newer and less familiar style of living is a complex process and demands that an individual possess the skills and self-knowledge to create an appropriate support system for the change (Moos, 1976). As Morgan (1974) noted, a growing need has surfaced for group contexts designed to accommodate persons going through these kinds of life stages or transitions.

The vast majority of life transition groups focus on helping people deal with the unexpected. It is dramatic, unanticipated transitions, catalyzed by personal loss, that are most shocking to an individual. Transition groups attempt to provide a mechanism for successfully resolving these important life changes. Among the significant life transitions that many people struggle with are: (1) adjusting to the death of a life mate, a family member, or other; (2) making a major career change; (3) learning to cope with an uncorrectable physical injury; (4) leaving the family and entering the adult world; and (5) creating a new way of life following the breakup of a primary relationship.

CORE ELEMENTS. The degree of structure employed in life transition groups varies widely, and, therefore, they have fewer core components in common than do life skill and life theme groups. A first major commonality of life transition groups is that they are change oriented and the change goal is identified and openly shared. As noted above, life transition groups offer vehicles for negotiating changes that become necessary because of some psychological or physical loss or result from self-willed alterations in one's life situation. Second, they focus on building future styles of relating based upon a clear understanding of how the past has led to one's present status. Last, life transition groups are time limited. The typical length of a group ranges from four to ten sessions.

LEADER BEHAVIORS AND SKILLS.   In life transition groups, the leader is only moderately active and is highly dependent on the healing and nurturing forces present within the group members to help participants effect integration and readjustment. The leader goes beyond the boundaries of traditional group counseling by using structure to augment and promote the change process. Thus, the development and facilitation of a life transition group is both an art and a rational process.

Because a life transition group requires that a leader be aware simultaneously of the emotional needs of each member and their progress toward the desired change goal, it is particularly desirable for a prospective leader to first cofacilitate a group. The primary leader has a responsibility to "clinic" with the cofacilitator (trainee) the progress of the group participants so that the cofacilitator can gain skill in recognizing the critical incidents and points of transitional movement occurring during the life of the group.

DESIGNING A STRUCTURED GROUP

The next three chapters in this work describe existing structured groups designed to help an individual acquire a life skill, examine a life theme, and effectively resolve an important life transition. Each of the programs can be implemented in a wide variety of settings without need for significant revision.

Even though the structured groups to be presented are fairly comprehensive, many people may still desire to create their own type of group. To assist in this process of designing new kinds of structured groups, a series of conceptual and practical guidelines is presented here. For purposes of clarity and ease of application they have been divided into three areas: (1) pregroup planning, (2) group format consideration, and (3) evaluation of outcome. In designing a structured group it is critical to give attention to each of these three areas, as all are important to the effectiveness of a structured group.

Pregroup Planning Variables

The four key conceptual and practical preprogram variables are:

1. statement of purpose and focus of the group;
2. assessment of need for the group in the population being served;
3. determination of staff and supportive resources; and
4. development of a marketing strategy

The first step in the organization of a structured group is to articulate as specifically as possible the goal or focus of the group. Once the aim of the group has been clarified, it is necessary to assess the need for that type of group in the agency, institution, or community where it is to be offered. Assessment procedures do not have to be intricate or elaborate, since the purpose is simply to forecast response and identify target groups. Often the need for a particular type of structured group can be determined by (1) intensive interviews with a small number of people; (2) review of the types of problems presented to your agency or prevalent within the community; (3) a brief questionnaire given to a representative sample of the population being served; or (4) research data reported in books and journals on developmental needs of people in the age range you serve.

After identifying the need for the group being developed, the next important task is to match existing resources to the degree of need. Developing, implementing, and revising structured groups requires a significant time commitment. For example, it may be necessary for staff members to upgrade or embellish their group skills. Staff members also need to learn how to tap the resources of the institution or community since many structured groups may be offered outside of the sponsoring agency or may require the use of equipment (videotape and the like).

The final preprogram planning variable is marketing the group to potential consumers. Active marketing aimed at increasing the visibility of the group is important, particularly where the clientele are unfamiliar with the structured developmental group concept. It must be remembered that structured groups represent attempts to intervene before unmet normal developmental needs deteriorate into deeper psychological troubles. While counselors providing traditional forms of counseling and therapy can rely upon the duress experienced by clients with severe problems to motivate them to seek assistance, leaders of structured groups cannot. A significant portion of the clientele being served by structured groups is not deeply troubled emotionally and thus must be motivated to participate through other means.

Group Format Considerations

Before the actual formation of a structured group several important issues related to group format must be considered. They are:

1. elaboration of the goal;
2. specification of major program elements;

3. identification of objectives and selection of appropriate exercises and techniques;
4. provision of opportunity of reality testing; and
5. determination of size, duration, and membership.

If the four pregroup planning steps have been effectively carried out, then the groundwork has been laid to determine the actual format of the group.

The first step in developing an appropriate format is to clarify further the goal of the group. The group facilitator must be able to explain in nontechnical language to the members the precise goal they will be trying to achieve and how the achievement of the goal can make a difference in their lives. The participants should understand clearly what will change. For example, will the focus be on eliminating specific counterproductive behaviors? On clarifying life values? On learning how to be appropriately assertive? The facilitator should be able to provide some positive descriptions of the behavior or attitudes of people who have acquired the life skill or resolved the life theme in this particular type of structured group. In addition, it is important that the group facilitator help each member personalize the group goal. For example, it is not enough simply to state that this group will be dealing with a specific goal, such as becoming more assertive. The person must be able to identify how the group can help him or her with his/her specific assertion deficit. Will the individual learn to become less aggressive? Will the group help the person become more goal directed in asking for what he/she needs? Will the individual learn to defend his/her rights? In other words, what the group can do for each participant needs to be spelled out clearly.

The second step in developing a format designed to achieve a stated goal is to specify key program components and indicate how they relate to the overall purpose of the group. For example, in designing an assertion training group, it would be necessary to indicate what the components of assertive behavior are (such as eye contact, body posture, vocal tone, timing, and goal directedness) and the ways a person could use assertive skills (to defend against verbal attack, to express positive feelings, etc.). In helping a person acquire a life skill, understand a vital theme, or effect a desired transition, it is necessary to identify the individual steps involved in building cumulatively toward the successful attainment of the goal.

A third necessary step is to select appropriate group exercises or techniques and arrange them so that the growth or discovery process unfolds sequentially, builds cumulatively on previous learning, maintains motivation through minimizing frustration and maximizing enjoyment, and achieves the goal in the most efficient amount of time.

Fourth, it is critically important that the facilitator provide an opportunity for each participant to test his/her new learning—a new attitude, skill, or direction in life—in the group. A group setting is an ideal environment for reality testing, seeking support, or trying to approximate a desired behavior. Honest feedback from group members helps the individual to operationalize new learnings and increases the likelihood that these learnings can be utilized outside the group.

After the group facilitator has clearly elaborated the goal, specified the basic elements of the learning process, selected appropriate techniques and exercises, and made provisions for reality testing, the next step is to determine the desired size, duration, and membership characteristics of the group. The size will depend upon the amount of individualization the facilitator must provide each member. The more individual attention each member of the group is to receive, the smaller the group size must be. In general, life skills and life transition groups are limited to twelve people or less, while life theme groups can be expanded to accommodate any number of persons. The number of sessions and duration of each will vary according to the goal and size of the group. Life transition and life skills groups usually meet for several sessions on a weekly basis, while some life theme groups meet only once or twice altogether. Many group facilitators report that multiple sessions produce the most satisfactory and lasting results.

An important format consideration is the establishment of criteria for the selection of appropriate group participants. Of course, the basic criterion for inclusion is commonness of some specific need (to become assertive, overcome grief, clarify values), and all participants should have some degree of need to achieve the group's stated goal. It is also important that a potential member not be so burdened with psychological problems that his/her inclusion in the group will detract significantly from the ability of other group members to gain from the group experience. In order to insure that a potential member is appropriately motivated and equipped to profit from the experience, facilitators sometimes prefer to hold a short screening interview with each prospective client. This pre group screening session can be used to explain the nature of the group and to assess the potential member's motivational level. This is particularly true of groups that involve multiple sessions such as life skills groups.

Evaluation of Effectiveness

Evaluation of structured groups has some direct parallels with research on other modes of counseling and therapy. The fact that the experience of theory and practice is more advanced than the ability to assess behavior change adequately applies both to psychotherapeutic strategies and outcomes and to structured group methods. The major difference is that because structured groups are fairly recent developments, they have not been the subject of as many research studies as have other more traditional forms of helping services.

A second parallel with research on group counseling in general is found in the few empirical studies done to date on structured groups. The preponderance of studies has led to a single, usually immediate, subjective self-report assessment completed at the end of the group program or shortly thereafter. This type of study has the dual purpose of providing feedback to the group leader for improvement of further groups and of measuring the participants' view of the group's effectiveness in helping them accomplish their desired goal. The results of the majority of these studies based on the participants feedback indicate that they feel positive about their accomplishment of the stated goal. Less common, but more desirable methodologically, are those few studies that measure "gains" within a single group through some pre- and postscheme of measurement of change. Finally, although all too infrequent in group studies of any nature, are those research studies that evaluate treatment outcomes by comparison with various types of control groups. This lack of well-controlled research is evident also in the evaluation of the effectiveness of one-to-one counseling, for practitioners rarely conduct any systematic empirical assessment of their clients' experience in therapy.

Overall, the current state of evaluation of structured groups can be characterized as sparse and predominantly superficial—which is not surprising, considering its neophyte status. To date, the most thorough research has been undertaken in life skills groups, and most notably in assertive skills training. Even here, however, work on evaluation is as yet only beginning to move toward being useful and of high quality. Most often methodological weaknesses characterize the research, particularly with regard to insufficient numbers of subjects studied, inappropriate or totally absent comparisons with control groups, or inadequate assessment devices. Some studies do employ behavioral outcome measures and appropriate valid and reliable inventories; but these are few in number, of recent origin, and primarily accomplished with college student populations. However, the fact that these studies are beginning to surface can be taken as a sign of the increasing maturity of the structured group movement.

Generally, more sophisticated studies with matched control groups are needed to determine the efficacy of the structured groups, and evaluation needs to be done at longer posttreatment intervals so that designers of similar programs have a scientific basis for relating program elements to outcomes. In this light, it would be helpful if component parts of the various format models were isolated and analyzed, including conceptual variables and their operational measures. Even though few well-controlled research efforts have been made as yet, the situation can still be viewed as promising. With the advent of these structured developmental groups, the opportunities for research and development of alternative modes of counseling assistance are plentiful. Also, as they grow in number and expand in scope and method of delivery, there appears to be reasonable cause for optimism over their future, both as effective modes of providing service, and as objects of empirical evaluation. For example, a review of the recent literature on assertion skills training groups reveals that clear-cut, positive results have been obtained, particularly where behavioral measures and controlled studies have been employed.

In addition to empirical measurement of the extent to which group members achieve their desired goals, leaders of structured groups should continue to utilize participants' feedback as a basis for possible revision of the group format. Because goals are clearly identified and learning builds cumulatively from one session to the next, structured groups do have some degree of built-in accountability. For instance, if a group member is having difficulty achieving a goal, it becomes readily apparent to her/himself, the facilitator, and other group members. An examination of the particular activity being used to meet the stipulated objective is probably in order.

As noted previously, although some controlled research studies have been conducted, the most common form of outcome measure used to date is feedback from the participants through interviews or questionnaires. Any attempt to assess the impact of a component of a structured group on an individual should be detailed enough to identify the elements which lead to success or the lack of it. Thus, feedback should be solicited from group members with regard to:

1. clarity and appropriateness of the goal;
2. what information contributed to the achievement of the goal;
3. helpfulness or limitations of the particular exercises used;
4. the size and length of the group;
5. adequacy of opportunity for reality testing;
6. extent of generalization to everyday living; and
7. stability of learning, particularly with time.

The group facilitator should also evaluate the effectiveness of the group from the leader's perspective. Did the group reach the desired target audience? Was the need properly estimated for the group in the population being served? Were appropriate members selected for inclusion in the group? Was the goal individualized in such a way that each group member was motivated to learn?

SUMMARY

In this chapter, the three major conceptual categories of structured groups and their respective core components have been presented. These conceptual bench marks are also the prototypical model for a structured developmental group of any type. In addition, descriptions of several practical steps useful in designing such a developmental group experience were outlined, and the status and needs for evaluation described. In the next chapter, definitions of specific life skills groups are elaborated, and several programs are outlined. This is followed by similar presentations for life theme groups and life transition groups. Life skills groups help persons to acquire the interpersonal skills necessary for effective functioning and satisfying living. This chapter describes nine group programs, with a brief outline for each, an overview of their aims and format, and the activities and objectives for each are given in some detail.

Chapter 3

LIFE SKILLS GROUPS

Life skills groups have as their common objective the development of life-enhancing skills which enable people to cope successfully with the psychological demands of everyday living. Basically, they try to help people fill in specific developmental gaps that may have occurred during their lifetime, or, ideally, teach appropriate skills as needed. Specifically, they help individuals acquire the interpersonal skills and abilities that are considered essential to successful negotiation of everyday tasks and interactions.

The goal of a specific type of life skills groups can be quite broad or very narrow. For example, consider the differences in scope of life skills groups designed to help people learn to control and eliminate feelings of anxiety. Some anxiety management groups are designed to relieve a full range of anxiety-based problems, including somatic complaints, social concerns, or general feelings of anxiety; while others are designed to relieve a single manifestation of anxiety such as at public speaking or test taking situations. Usually, the more comprehensive life skills groups require a large number of sessions to achieve the stated goal successfully. This chapter focuses mainly on providing descriptions of broad-scope life skills programs, since they often encompass the key elements of the more narrowly focused groups.

Structured life skills groups have some common methods, techniques, and procedures that are considered to be essential regardless of the wide variety and particular emphasis of the group. The core elements were described more fully in Chapter 2. Each one of the elements listed below is usually a key part of any life skills group:

1. a clearly identified focus or goal;
2. development of responsiveness (intentionality);
3. use of an education–experiential format (including exercises and techniques);
4. criteria for preselection of group members;
5. concern for establishing a positive, cohesive group atmosphere; and
6. a predetermined number of sessions.

FOCUS OF LIFE SKILLS GROUPS

The majority of life skills programs currently being offered attempt to foster the developmental process in two basic ways. First, many life skills groups advance the development of critical skills which most people acquire only incompletely during their adolescent years, such as (a) the inability to manage the anxiety that accompanies increasing responsibility and independence; (b) the difficulty in negotiating needs and asserting effectively; (c) the lack of interpersonal skills which limit the ability to communicate intimately and clearly; and (d) the need to learn to integrate more fully life and work goals.

Second, life skills groups facilitate the growth process by providing a structured experience which allows people to develop specific life-enhancing behaviors and to eliminate self-defeating actions. Examples of the needs addressed by life skills groups in this category are:

1. developing effective parenting skills;
2. reducing excessive weight;
3. improving sleeping habits;
4. controlling smoking habits; and
5. developing creative decision-making skills.

Descriptions of Life Skills Programs

The nine structured groups described below were selected from a large number of programs because they represent models which are either comprehensive in scope or have achieved fairly widespread use. For each of the nine groups a capsule description of the developmental issue is presented, a general overview of the specific program illustrated is given, and a detailed description of the activities and objectives of each group session is outlined. In addition, we have identified the originator(s) of each model and have presented a session-by-session description of the activities and objectives as it was submitted to us. Therefore, the style of description of each program varies, as well as the degree of detail used to elaborate upon the activities employed. One major variation among the nine structured group models presented relates to the way the objectives of each session are reported. Some models identify an objective for each group activity within a session. Other structured groups utilize several exercises or activities to achieve a specific objective. In situations where there is not a one-to-one correspondence between an activity and specific objective, the overall objectives for each session are listed at the beginning of each session description.

The reader should take into account the fact that each of the programs reported was condensed by the original developer(s) to conform to our format requirements. In some cases leader manuals, workbooks, and other materials had to be reduced from over 50 to approximately 10 pages. Readers of this work are encouraged to write directly to the individual program developers for more complete information and supportive materials that would be helpful for effective program implementation. A list of these developers will be found at the end of the book on pages 277–280.

Anxiety Management Groups

The need to monitor, control, and eliminate unnecessary and often crippling feelings of anxiety is a task that confronts an increasing number of people in our "future shock" pace of living. The inability to manage the physical and psychological feelings of tension and anxiety that are present in daily living can dramatically influence the amount of enjoyment and satisfaction that a person experiences. Indeed, it is striking to note the degree to which people restrict their life styles and adopt many self-defeating behaviors to avoid having to cope with feelings of anxiety.

Structured groups designed to help people monitor and control feelings of anxiety are attempts to supply people with adaptive coping skills so that they will not have to rely on maladaptive coping styles. A wide variety of anxiety management groups has been devised over the past few years. As noted before, some group models focus on the treatment of a particular type of anxiety, while others are more comprehensive in scope. The model illustrated in detail in this chapter is a comprehensive model designed to deal with feelings of generalized anxiety, somatic complaints, speech and test-taking anxiety, free-floating anxiety, and many other manifestations of underlying tension.

ANXIETY MANAGEMENT TRAINING BY BARRY MCCARTHY.   The Anxiety Management Training model presented below was developed by Barry McCarthy in the Counseling Center at The American University, Washington, D. C. The group meets for one and one-half hours weekly for four weeks. Its purpose is to help people develop the skills to monitor and control nonproductive feelings of anxiety. The group relies largely upon behavioral concepts and is designed for eight to twelve participants. Since the group model utilizes progressive relaxation techniques, the leader must arrange for a comfortable room in which participants can recline on a soft surface (pillows or carpeting), where noise level can be controlled, and lighting can be dimmed at appropriate times.

The group participants can differ with regard to the type of anxiety-based problem they are experiencing. However, people who have developed several anxiety or phobic problems are considered inappropriate for participation. Because the group meets for one and one-half hours for four consecutive weeks, before joining the group each participant should agree to attend each session and do the homework assignments.

Group Format. The Anxiety Management Training model developed by McCarthy is a sequential skill-building approach. The concepts, exercises, time limits, and objectives are presented below.

SESSION 1

Activities	*Objectives*
1. Introduction and background (30–45 min.). a. Each person introduces him/herself	(1) to begin to establish group cohesiveness; (2) to obtain commitment to all four sessions; (3) to clarify how to learn to control and monitor anxiety;

Activities	*Objectives*
and states purpose for being in group.	(4) through buddy system to have contact with person outside group who monitors and reinforces the person for practicing skill; (5) to begin to develop skills in relaxation, and to increase participants' feelings that they can learn to manage and eliminate nonproductive tension.
b. Leader gets verbal commitment from each person to do homework; describes group format (including confidentiality); sets up buddy system; explains theory and technique of relaxation; stresses the goal of monitoring and controlling anxiety (importance of self-control); explains the difference between anxiety management training and hypnosis, meditation, yoga, etc.; and gives clinical and personal examples	

Activities   *Objectives*

of when it can
be used.

2. Practice of relaxation
   exercises (30–45
   min.).
3. Discussion of
   exercises and
   homework (15 min.).
   Leader reemphasizes
   that relaxation is a
   skill which must be
   practiced to be
   learned, and that one
   must learn to
   discriminate between
   tension and various
   degrees of
   relaxation.
4. Homework
   assignments:
   a. Practice
      exercises a
      minimum of
      once a day for
      ten minutes
      each. Practice
      tensing muscles
      first, eyes closed,
      comfortable
      position.
   b. Keep list of what
      makes you
      anxious during
      week. Try to
      discriminate

Activities

where anxiety is felt.

c. Check with buddy at least once during week to monitor progress.

SESSION 2

1. Check on homework (10–15 min.). Important to be sure that buddy system is positively reinforcing and that person is ready to make maximal use of relaxation exercises this session.

2. Discuss use of imagery and development of relaxation and competency scenes (30 min.). Provide the following guidelines:

   a. Since anxiety is an internally cued response, it can be elicited and controlled and the procedure

Objectives

(1) to insure that group members are completing homework assignments and acquiring relaxation skills; (2) to begin to develop the capacity to utilize imagery as a way of controlling anxiety; (3) to further refine the skill of relaxation and use it to monitor and control feelings of tension.

Activities	*Objectives*

learned and practiced via use of imagery.

b. It is important to use all senses, including touch, sight, hearing, movement, smell, etc., while imagining scenes.

c. See self directly in scene, not a picture.

d. Each participant is to construct a relaxation scene. Examples: lying on beach, having back rubbed, skiing, etc.

e. Each participant is to construct a competency (mastery) scene. Examples: boss saying "Good job," cooking gourmet meal, getting an "A," etc.

3. Practice relaxation exercises (30 min.).

4. While still relaxed, each

Activities	*Objectives*

member turns on
relaxation and
competency scenes,
each scene twice for
one minute each.

5. Discuss relaxation
and imagery
experience and ways
to make them more
real and vivid.

6. Homework
assignments:
  a. Practice
relaxation for
same time
periods, but by
end of week
fade out
technique of
tensing before
relaxing.
  b. While relaxed,
use relaxation
and competency
scenes to
enhance the
vividness and
comfort.
  c. Begin thinking
of two anxiety-
provoking
scenes. Scene
should be
focused where
individual

Activities	*Objectives*
is feeling anxiety, so that it is out of control.	

   d. Meet with buddy at least once to reinforce practice and monitor progress.

7. End session by taking.5 minutes to relax group (without first tensing) and then imagine relaxation and competency scenes. Participants must practice and refine this during week.

SESSION 3

1. Discuss homework and practice on relaxation and imagery (10–15 min.).	(1) to insure that each member feels comfortable and skilled in his/her ability to relax and use imagery; (2) to teach the procedures and concepts involved in using anxiety management skills; (3) to practice anxiety management techniques; (4) to be sure that each member understands and accepts the procedures; (5) to
2. Each person constructs two anxiety scenes (20–30 min.).	
3. Discuss concepts and procedures of anxiety	

Activities	*Objectives*
management training procedures (10–15 min.). Participants	make sure that each person has identified his/her own unique anxiety-cueing experience; (6) to enable participants to reach a relaxed state without first using muscle tension techniques.

Activities

management training procedures (10–15 min.). Participants

a. recognize that the goal is to learn to monitor and control anxiety;

b. use anxiety as a cue to introduce feelings of relaxation and/or competency; and

c. signal leader by raising right index finger.

4. Anxiety Management Training (30–40 min.).

Important to reinforce that clients are learning to monitor and control anxiety. If participant signals anxiety, make sure he/she is relaxed before representing scene and present it for a shorter time. Hopefully, both anxiety scenes will be finished during session.

Objectives

make sure that each person has identified his/her own unique anxiety-cueing experience; (6) to enable participants to reach a relaxed state without first using muscle tension techniques.

Activities	*Objectives*
a. First three scene presentations. Participants are to feel the anxiety, become aware of physical and psychological manifestations of anxiety (20-sec. presentation).	
b. Each anxiety scene followed by 45 seconds of relaxation with either relaxation or competency scene. Members learn to replace anxiety with relaxation. Be sure participants are relaxed before presenting anxiety scene again.	
c. For the remaining presentations, goal is for participants to be relaxed during anxiety scene, i.e.,	

Activities   *Objectives*

to be able to
imagine anxiety
scene for 45 sec.
without anxiety.
Present at 20,
25, 30, and
finally 45 sec.
Goal achieved
when no one in
group signals
feeling of
anxiety with two
45-second
presentations.

5. Discuss procedure
   and homework
   (10–20 min.).
6. Homework
   assignments:
   a. Practice scenes
      at least twice at
      home, in relaxed
      comfortable
      position, eyes
      closed. Then
      practice anxiety-
      inducing scene
      twice in real-
      life situation.
   b. Practice relaxing
      with eyes open,
      and then in
      regular, not
      comfortable
      position.

Activities   *Objectives*

Eventual goal is
to be able to
relax in
real-world
situation.

c. Be aware of
other
situations in
which anxiety
management can
be used.

d. Check with
buddy at least
once during
week.

SESSION 4

1. Discuss homework
(10–15 min.).
Start with success
experiences and then
move to problem
situations. In
comparing to real
life situations, leader
should emphasize
taking small steps; if
anxious, moving back
a step or two until
relaxed, and not
letting anxiety
snowball but finding
that it can be
monitored and
controlled.

2. Participants practice

(1) to troubleshoot any
homework problems; (2) to
work toward further generalization of anxiety management skills; (3) to make sure
each member has the ability
to relax quickly and naturally; (4) to provide more
training and reinforcement
in anxiety management
techniques; (5) to encourage and support continued
practices of skill.

Activities   *Objectives*

anxiety management
technique, develop
two new scenes
(15–20 min.).
  a. One scene
     should be a
     troublesome
     situation, and
     increase anxiety
     evocation.
  b. The second
     scene should be
     another problem
     area where the
     client would like
     to feel more
     relaxed and
     competent.
3. Use of the Anxiety
    Management
    Training Technique
    (30–40 min.).
    Same procedures as
    in third session.
4. General discussion of
    continued use of
    anxiety management
    techniques and
    continued use of
    self-control
    procedures to
    monitor and control
    anxiety.
  a. Continued
     practice of
     anxiety

Activities	*Objectives*
management at home both in imagery and real life situation.	

b. Continued practice of relaxation in real-life situation, dropping out relaxation "props."

c. In new anxiety situations, using imagery and anxiety management techniques.

d. Meeting with buddy in two weeks to discuss continued use of program.

Assertion Training Groups

One of the most universally recognized and desired needs of people is to be effectively assertive. In one respect, our culture requires us to give feedback, receive feedback, and initiate interaction with others, and demands the ability to be assertive. However, in another respect our cultural patterns prescribe certain behaviors or ways of relating to others which conflict with the development of assertive skills. Since the need for a person to be able to assert is high and the chances for acquisition of the skill are rather low, the overwhelming public response to participation in assertion training programs is not surprising.

Structured groups designed to enable people to develop effective assertive behavior range from short one-session models to those that spread training over six or more consecutive weeks. The longer training models have produced the most lasting benefits to the participant. This is not to say, however, that the one- and two-session models are without value. These shorter models seem to be very effective in raising individuals' awareness of their needs of assertive skills, as well as providing a forum for their resolution. In addition, they often help a person learn to identify the common mistakes made by many nonassertive and aggressively nonassertive people.

ASSERTION TRAINING BY DOLPH PRINTZ.   The structured group program selected for inclusion in this chapter is entitled "Assertion Training" and was developed by Dolph Printz in the office of Counseling and Student Development at the University of Rhode Island, Kingston. The model is an intensive assertive training experience designed for a relatively small number of participants. The ideal number should not exceed eight (plus two trainers) and should consist of both sexes. The purpose of limiting the group to eight participants is to insure adequate time for role-playing and behavioral rehearsal. The cotrainers must be assertive individuals in their own right and preferably be one male and one female. The program includes six weekly sessions besides prescreening interviews and a follow-up session one month after the end of the sixth session. Each session lasts two hours, and all sessions are scheduled consecutively. Videoptape equipment may be used during the second, third, fourth, and fifth sessions. Although there are some highly desirable advantages to using videotape, it is not mandatory.

Before the beginning of the first session each participant will have had a short prescreening interview by one of the group leaders, the goals of which are: (1) to validate the fact that the prospective participant lacks assertive skills; (2) to explain the group format, goals, and meeting schedule; (3) to obtain the client's commitment to attend all sessions and complete homework assignments; and (4) to screen out clients for whom the group may be inappropriate. Once six appropriate participants have been selected, Printz outlines the following sequence of activities and objectives for his assertion training model:

SESSION 1.

Activities	Objectives
1. Trainees and group members introduce themselves.	1. Begin to establish a sense of group cohesiveness.
2. Trainers hand out outline of principles and activitiies for first session. (This is done for all sessions.)	2. Clients then have a guideline for the session that reduces some of the anticipating anxiety and becomes a reference sheet for later review.
3. Trainers explain rationale for behavioral therapy in general, and assertive training in particular.	
4. Trainers explain that the skill of assertive behavior can be broken down into manageable behavioral components; such as	4. This introduces the "components" section which operationalizes the skills acquisition.

Activities

a. eye contact and
   appropriate
   facial
   expression;
b. body posture
   and appropriate
   hand
   movements;
c. vocal tone,
   volume, and
   quality; and
d. goal
   directedness.

5. After each
   presentation of a
   behavioral
   component, the
   trainers model the
   contrast between
   ineffective and
   effective use of that
   component. Group
   members then pair
   up and alternately
   perform a related
   exercise. For
   example, the exercise
   to follow the eye
   contact component
   has one person
   beginning a
   conversation (content
   irrelevant) with his
   partner while looking
   at the floor;

Objectives

5. Essentially, this and
   the following
   exercises are
   interpersonal
   warm-ups but they
   also allow the
   individuals to exercise
   the behavioral
   contrast in themselves
   and others. These
   should be enjoyable
   above all.

Activities	*Objectives*
gradually he makes full eye contact and continues speaking.	
6. Trainers present assertive guide-line: "State the feeling that needs to be expressed as clearly as possible, and state what you need from the other person. If appropriate, ask for respect from the other person for your feelings."	6. This statement is intended only to be a clear statement of the general interpersonal mechanics of assertion. The last sentence reflects that the asserter does not always get the goal he/she wants, but always has the human right to express his/her feeling or opinion.
7. Trainers present reasons for assertion: a. Objective approach assertion is assertive behavior utilized in the pursuit of or movement toward an objective goal (e.g., asking for a pay raise, asking to borrow an object from a friend, getting past rude secretaries or	7. This breakdown of the definition of assertion allows for a clearer conceptionalization of assertive motives and provides group members with a cognitive model for their assertion skills.

Activities	*Objectives*
clerks to settle a matter, etc.).	
b. Subjective approach assertion is assertive behavior utilized to approach another person for reasons of interpersonal attraction or any subjective communication to another person (e.g., getting beyond superficial acquaintances to actual friendships, communicating interpersonal feelings, etc.).	b. This type of assertive behavior is often neglected and many programs focus on defensive assertions; it is important to include assertion that is directly life-enhancing.
c. Defensive assertion is assertive behavior utilized to maintain one's individual rights and personal dignity; in essence, one is "defending" one's life-space.	

Activities	*Objectives*
8. Trainers call for questions and clarify any issues that require it.	
9. Trainer-modeled role plays. Trainers role play three pairs of scenes, one pair for each of the three types of assertion, i.e., objective, subjective, and defensive. Format for trainer-modeled role plays:	9. This procedure models the basic role-play procedure which will be used with the group members. Essentially, group members see the process of behavioral shaping toward effective assertive behavior.
a. Trainers utilize three preselected situations to correspond with the three types of assertion.	
b. They first assign behavior component discrimination roles to each of the group members who then critique the role plays after the first scene of a pair. The discrimination roles are	b. This procedure allows for active group member practice in discrimination of behavioral components and for consolidation of modeled behavior.

	Activities	*Objectives*

Activities

for observation
of eye contact,
facial
expression, body
posture, hand
movements,
vocal tone and
quality, and
content (goal
directedness).
These roles
should be
rotated at the
end of each pair
of scenes.

c. Trainers first
play a scene with
the "asserter"
being
unassertive by
leaving out some
components (1
min).

d. Group members
critique presence
or absence of
components.

e. Trainers replay
same scene with
effective
assertive
behaviors (1
min.).

e. Trainers are here
modeling
responses to
group feedback.

10. Homework
assignments:

a. Observe a

a. This observation

Activities	*Objectives*
good assertive role and study his/her behavioral components.	allows for further modeling effect.
b. In interactions with others, be aware of your own behavioral components and actively bring them into play in order to make better contact.	b. This assignment maintains clients' awareness of these components during the week and encourages them to flex their "body language" muscles.
c. Describe two situations in your own life in which you have been unable to be assertive and would like to be. Bring these written scenes to the next session.	c. These are the two basic scripts for individuals' role plays in the group. By using their own real-life situations, the group members are better able to generalize the group-learned skills to their lives.
d. Read selected articles or chapters on the "rights to be assertive."	

SESSION 2

1. Discussion of homework and sharing of past	1. Trainers can respond to group members' assertion-related

Activities

week's experiences.

2. Trainers hand out session outline.
3. Trainers explain some further behavioral guidelines for assertion:
   a. Relax as fully as possible before entering a difficult assertion situation. Group members can either be taught a quick relaxation technique in the group (such as Fensterheim's method) or be offered relaxation training at another time.
   b. Try to engage the other person from the beginning of an encounter with nonverbal behavioral components.
   c. Keep the goal of the interaction in mind

Objectives

experiences and positively reinforce any progress made. Also, individuals usually raise questions and issues that need to be dealt with.

a. It is clear that reducing one's anxiety before a difficult encounter is beneficial, and a relaxation technique is a valuable tool to possess.

b. Focusing on the very beginning of an assertive encounter is very important; initial contact is essential.

c. Persistence counts for a lot in assertion, and it

Activities	*Objectives*
and actively return to it when necessary.	may be necessary to "recycle" back to the goal.
d. Focus on getting your own feelings across in a direct, straightforward manner.	d. Since unassertive people worry excessively about the other person's feelings, it is reasonable at this point to encourage group members to devote more energy to their own feelings.
4. Trainer–client role plays: Half the group role plays the less difficult of their two written scenes with one of the trainers as the "assertee." Format for trainer–client role plays:	4. Starting with the less difficult allows for higher probability of initial success. Trainers should role play a character difficult enough to make the person work at the assertion, but not so much that the member is discouraged.
a. After group member describes his situation in enough detail to allow realistic role playing, he/she and	a. At this point, it is best to have a trainer in the "assertee" role (until perhaps the fourth session); the trainer can better modulate

Activities	*Objectives*
one of the trainers play it (about 1–2 min.).	degree of the resistance and general difficulty of the scene.
b. Immediately after the scene, the "asserter" views the videotape playback and critiques the behavioral components. If videotape is not available, then the group members can critique the "asserter's" use of behavioral components.	b. Group member actively observes and critiques his/her own behavior; the person "owns" his/her behavior.
c. One of the trainers initiates other group feedback and positive reinforcement. Suggestions are offered.	c. Trainers are here modeling a constructive reinforcement process.
d. The scene is played again as before with videotape and group feedback. If necessary,	d. This is basically a behavior-shaping procedure with a considerable amount of appropriate

Activities	*Objectives*
the process can be repeated a third time until the individual is comfortable with his/her performance and the group (and trainers) feels that progress has been made.	reinforcement. The trainers should be vigilant that group feedback is constructive and not hostile.

5. Homework assignments:

   a. Practice the quick relaxation technique when feeling anxious (or acquire other relaxation skills if desired).

b. Members now make a behavioral contract with the group to be accomplished during the week; i.e., to express their feelings in a specific nonthreatening situation.	b. This assignment begins a series of between-session contracts to motivate group members to change their behavior outside the group. These are "gentleman's agreements," but the demand characteristics of the group are a powerful motivating force.

SESSION 3

Activities	*Objectives*
1. Discussion and sharing of experiences and contracts.	1. It is hoped that group members have garnered their own positive reinforcement in vivo, but the group reinforcement is also beneficial.
a. Trainers (and group) actively and positively reinforce gains made.	a. This distinction is best made within role-play feedback, but a formal conceptual statement is helpful.
b. Broken contracts should be explored and suggestions made (non-punitively).	
2. Trainers hand out session outline.	
3. Trainers present three additional behavioral guidelines:	
a. Good assertion is not aggression; assertion should respect both the rights of the asserter and assertee.	

Activities	*Objectives*
Aggressive behavior clearly closes off communication of any really productive sort.	
b. Timing of an assertive response is critical in two respects:	
(1) When an individual does not assert in a given situation over time, he/she builds up anger and resentment which sometimes is then "dropped" much later on the other person; this delayed response is generally distorted and definitely nonproductive.	(1) Since many nonassertive people sometimes "explode" after a long period of silence, this concept allows them to see the connection between continued nonassertion and consequent eruptive aggression.
(2) Within an	(2) This concept

Activities

assertive encounter, the most effective response is an immediate response and the person should state his/her feeling before being sidetracked.

c. Before asserting, it is important that the individual internally reflect on the specific goal. The assertive response should begin with a personal feeling, very often initiating the interaction with "I . . ." By starting each assertive statement with the word "I," the trainer is encouraging the individual to

Objectives

is mostly elaborated in the role plays and emphasizes the first few moments of making contact with the other person.

c. This is emphasized to facilitate straightforward communication but also to prevent accusations of the other person which only serve to put others on the defensive.

Activities	*Objectives*
internally reflect on his/her purpose for asserting; that is, what really is the goal?	
4. Role plays with the second half of the group as described in Session 2.	
5. Homework assignment:	
a. Group members contract to act on a specific, real-life objective approach assertion (use same procedure as indicated in Session 2).	a. This second contract is more difficult than the previous one (Session 2), and with the later two contracts (Sessions 4 and 5) the hierarchy of increasing behavioral challenge is completed.

SESSION 4

1. Discussion and sharing of contracts (procedure indicated in Session 3).	1. The general objectives of the fourth and fifth sessions are identical to those reported in the second and third sessions.

Activities

2. Trainers hand out session outline.
3. Trainers review principles covered in past sessions (briefly) and respond to issues raised.
4. Role playing with group members, second scene (half the group).
5. Homework assignment:
   a. Group members contract to act on a specific real-life defensive assertion (same procedure as indicated in Session 2).

Objectives

3. This is intended as a conceptual refresher prior to the second go-around of role playing.

SESSION 5

1. Discussion and sharing of contracts (as before).
2. Trainers hand out session outline.
3. Role playing with second half of group.
4. Homework assignment:
   a. Group members

Activities   *Objectives*

contract for a
specific real-life
subjective
approach
assertion (as
before).

SESSION 6

1. Discussion and
   sharing of contracts
   (as before).
2. Group improvisa-
   tional role plays:
   a. Trainers and   a. These role plays
      group members   are intended as
      pick random   additional
      assertive   behavioral
      situations to role   practice and as
      play; these   enjoyment. These
      should be   sudden situations
      situations which   are frequent in
      occur suddenly   life and require
      and for which an   spontaneous
      asserter must   assertive
      respond without   responses.
      prior rehearsal
      or planning
      (e.g., someone
      steps in front of
      you in line,
      someone takes
      your seat,
      people talk
      loudly at movies,
      etc.).

Activities	*Objectives*
b. As many of the group can get involved as possible so that the situation is realistic; one person is targeted as the "asserter."	
c. Videotape is not used for these role plays, and feedback and reinforcement are chiefly in the hands of the group.	
d. The scene may be replayed as necessary.	
3. Troubleshooting and wrap-up.	
4. Announcement of time and date of Session 7 (approximately one month later).	4. The purpose of the follow-up session is to allow the clients "time in the field"; the delayed final session can address problems which have been encountered and utilize additional specialized role plays.
5. Homework assignments:	
a. Keep a continuous	a. The diary allows the clients to

Activities	*Objectives*
assertive diary for the coming month with entries for as many situations as can be charted; emphasis can be on both the positive occurrences and the problematic skill areas.	self-document his/her own success areas and also to delineate the situations or skills which need further work.
b. Immediately before Session 7, review the diary and summarize the successful and problematic areas.	b. This review provides the basis for the troubleshooting work in the follow-up session.

SESSION 7

1. Trainers facilitate free-flowing discussion concerning clients' successes and problems with assertion. a. Role playing can be utilized to illustrate the	1. Since this session is essentially a "booster" session with emphasis on troubleshooting, there is no firm agenda.

Activities	*Objectives*
issues being discussed.	
b. The issue of choice in asser-tion can be intro-duced by the trainers if not raised by the group.	b. Although the behavioral tech-nology of assertion has been acquired, an individual has the right to choose whether or not he/she uses it in certain situations.
2. Trainers elicit feedback on their personal and program performance.	2. The goal of soliciting feedback is to learn what leader behaviors and/or activities group members felt were helpful or not helpful.
3. Good-bye.	

Communication Skills Groups

The ability to communicate clearly, openly, and with a feel-ing of naturalness is an attribute highly desired by many people. Unfortunately, people often concentrate more on the inadequacies in their communication of thoughts and feelings to others than they do on ways in which they can change their behavior to improve their ability to relate. A person with a deficit in interpersonal communications skills is usually painfully aware of the negative feelings such as alienation, isolation, and social discomfort that often ac-company this lack of skill.

Communication skills groups provide a series of struc-tured activities that enable people to develop effective interpersonal skills and rewarding styles of relating, as well as to overcome specific personal barriers to effective communication. The actual format of communication skills groups varies widely, from those that emphasize listening and responding skills to those that focus on reducing social anxiety and improving interpersonal transaction abilities.

Although communication skills groups vary considerably, they can be roughly categorized into two types. The first type is designed for the individual who has minimal, if any, relationships with others. He/she can be characterized as a person who has trouble initiating relationships with others, cannot sustain relationships, is inhibited in heterosexual relationships, and experiences general feelings of social anxiety. The second form of communication skills group is for people who have formed a relationship with another person and want to enhance the quality of that relationship. The following sections highlight an exemplary program in each category.

COMMUNICATION SKILLS WORKSHOP BY STAFF OF THE COUNSELING CENTER AT COLORADO ST. UNIV.   The Communication Skills Workshop (CSW) developed by the staff of the Counseling Center at Colorado State University, Fort Collins, is an example of the first type of program, that is, one designed to assist individuals to develop effective interpersonal relationships. It helps individuals who have difficulty initiating and sustaining relationships with other people. Despite its focus on the person whose interpersonal skills are inadequate, however, it can benefit a wide range of people. As indicated in the Communication Skills Workshop Manual, (1972) the purpose of this group is

> ... to provide an atmosphere in which members will learn and practice a model of good communication by increasing their ability to:
> 1.   be more honest and open about themselves (self-disclosure);

2. experience caring and being cared for (intimacy);
3. express their observations and reactions to other people (giving feedback);
4. hear and accept others' reactions to them (receiving feedback); and
5. identify and work toward new behavior (behavior change). (p. 1)

The general structure for the workshop is outlined on pages 1 and 2 of the Leader's Manual and is presented below:

The Communication Skills Workshop is a six-week session structured workshop with groups meeting once a week for 2 hours as well as one 7-hour session . . . Members also attend four weekly meetings with a smaller group between regular group sessions.
A. The Total Group
    1. Composition
        a. A CSW group should include seven to ten members, composed equally of men and women if possible.
        b. The authors found that combining participants with a variety of social skill levels into one group seemed to facilitate interaction and change.
        c. It is recommended that there be one male and one female facilitator although use of a single facilitator would probably be successful.
    2. Sessions
        a. The group will meet for seven sessions over the course of six weeks. With the exception of the second session, meetings are weekly and last 2 hours.
        b. The second session takes place during the week between the first and third sessions, and lasts 7 hours. Session 2 takes place on any available full day, such as a Saturday, from 9:00 A.M. to 4:00 P.M.
B. The Mini-Group
    1. Composition
        a. The mini-group is composed of three to four CSW participants, maintaining as equal a ratio of men to women as possible. At least one member of both sexes should be in each mini-group.

b. At least one member who has been determined by the facilitator to be potentially helpful, caring, or facilitative, and who is somewhat strong relative to the rest of the group should be in each mini-group.

c. The mini-group should be composed of participants whom the facilitators predict may be helpful to each other.

d. There is no facilitator present at mini-group meetings.

2. Sessions

a. Mini-groups meet during the week between sessions of the total group.

b. There are four mini-group meetings, beginning after Session 3, taking place weekly at a time convenient to the members of each individual mini-group.

c. There is no designated time limit for mini-group meetings.

By providing opportunities for large group interactions with the facilitator(s) present, small group interactions without a facilitator, and specific help with goal setting, the aim is to maximize the likelihood of positive change in interpersonal behavior.

Group Format. The Communication Skills Workshop model utilizes a sequential skill-building approach within a clearly articulated and specified format. A condensed version of the activities and objectives in the Communication Skills Workshop Manual is presented below. The effective implementation of this program will be greatly enhanced by direct use of the Leader's Manual which can be obtained from the Counseling Center at Colorado State University.

SESSION 1

Activities	*Objectives*
1. Introduction and expectation setting.	1. To provide participants with a general overview of

Activities	*Objectives*
	the workshop structure, clearly establish the facilitators as authority figures (i.e., knowledgeable about process).
a. Facilitator describes the general structure of the group, mentioning the weekly sessions, the all-day meeting, and the mini-group meetings.	
b. Facilitator stresses importance of a commitment to attend all sessions. Contracts are signed.	
2. Warm-up exercise. Name chant. The group repeats each member's name in two different ways, e.g., with joy and anger, sadness and humor.	2. To maximize the likelihood of remembering one another's name.
3. Nonverbal—creative objects. Group	3. To free people of self-consciousness

	Activities		*Objectives*
	members pass around three or four objects for which each participant creates a different use while the group guesses what it is, i.e., ruler, ball, pie tin, handkerchief.		from being in a strange setting by providing a fun activity and to give participants the chance to watch how people act nonverbally.
4.	Verbal communication—who am I?—and individual introductions. Participants write five key dimensions about themselves which are then pinned to the front of each participant. Participants circulate, read one another's papers while remaining silent. After the nonverbal phase the participants return to two or three different people they thought interesting and ask questions which they ordinarily would not ask. The participants then choose one member of the group	4.	To allow participants to become acquainted quickly in a relatively nonthreatening way; to look at and share with others who we are, what roles we have, and our own uniqueness.

Activities	*Objectives*
whom they introduce to the group by telling something about the individual not previously revealed.	
5. Trust exercise—trust fall. Participants form a small circle in which one member stands in the center. The person in the center, body rigid, arms at side, falls toward the circle. The members of the group catch and pass the center person around the circle. This entails passing the person across the diameter of the circle as well as around the circle.	5. To introduce the basic concept of trust.
6. Distribution of session-1 handout entitled, "Memo for Communication Skills Workshop," and end of first session.	6. The first session is intended to provide an opportunity for group participants to begin to feel comfortable with each other, and to reduce the anxiety usually shared at the beginning of groups. Group members

Activities	*Objectives*
	experience having fun together, they begin the process of self-disclosure in a gradual and controlled manner, and they are introduced to nonverbal exercises.

SESSION 2

1. Behavior description. Triads are formed and participants are given specific instructions for describing certain behaviors (15 min.) and processing reactions.	1. To practice describing nonverbal behavior objectively without interpretation; to study the body language messages that accompany verbalization; to alert group members to the array of signals which they emit when they are attempting to communicate.
2. Sharing important objects. Each member has been told to bring something to the group that is important and would help the group get to know him/her better. Participants show the	2. To have each group member share an important part of self with the group; to generate data about each member with respect to how much he/she shares and how he/she reacts with others.

Activities	*Objectives*
group what they have brought and explain why it is important to them. The group asks any questions they wish of each member. The group share spontaneously, rather than going around the circle. Discussion follows (30 min.).	
3. First impressions. One group member tells what part of nature he/she sees himself/herself as. This may be a flower, tree, animal, element, etc. The person tells why he/she sees himself/herself this way. Then he/she chooses another group member and tells what part of nature he/she sees that person as. The receiver of feedback tells why he/she thinks the description was chosen, and how he/she feels about it. The giver of	3. To focus on the processes of self-disclosure and feedback; to provide a rather nonthreatening, playful context in which individuals can give their honest impressions of each other.

Activities	*Objectives*
feedback then tells why he/she chose what he/she said. In this way, the feedback process of is modeled. The process is repeated for each member of the group. Discussion follows (1 hour).	
4. Feedback model and Johari window. The leader passes out the handouts on feedback and the Johari window, explains their connection, and answers any questions from the group.	4. To realize in a coherent theoretical way the concepts acted out in first impressions; to teach the feedback model so that it can be used as a basis for the future interaction in 'he group.
5. Group interaction (using same format of behavior description exercise used previously). Group breaks into triads. Person A talks about why he/she came to the group, what things he/she wanted help with, how he/she feels about self. Person B tells A what he/she	5. To encourage self-disclosing behavior; to focus on feelings and emotions; to model support and understanding; to foster a supportive climate in the group.

Activities	*Objectives*
heard A saying. Person C serves as observer of interaction between A and B. Introductions are made by each person by other two members of his/her triad. The focus is on feelings (45 min.).	
6. Lunch. Participants first pair up with new partners, and then leaders introduce exercise to group members. During lunch, group members feed each other. Pairing up, each one feeds the other after obtaining food for the other. After lunch, some quiet time is allowed for each person to think about what he/she has been experiencing, how he/she feels, what he/she has learned about self (1 hour, 30 min.).	
7. Unstructured group discussion. Designed to keep the focus on	7. To allow time for free exchange, develop group cohesion,

Activities	*Objectives*
here and now, and relationships and feelings between group members. Videotape is used to record discussion for playback in third session (1 hour).	model and use good feedback process.
8. Cradling. One group member lies down on the floor, others reach under and lift the person up, rock her/him gently, lift to a position over their heads, and lower her/him gently. Each group member takes turn (30 min.).	8. To build group closeness, to continue the feeling of group support, to encourage nonverbal caring.
9. Group fantasy. The group members lie on the floor, on their backs, with their heads together like spokes on a wheel. They are told they are about to embark on an expedition together—everything is ready and they are set to go. Then any group member can set the scene or describe what he/she	9. To get an indication of the stage of group life; to provide a fantasy means of learning about relationships within the group.

Activities	*Objectives*

sees in his/her
fantasy (15 min.).

10. A short explanation
of handouts is
presented that
highlights the
process of
behavior-change goal
settings (15 min.).

11. Relaxation using
Jacobsen's relaxation
technique (30 min.).

SESSION 3

1. Videotape exercise.
Selected portions of
videotaped
interaction are
played back and
group members
watch. They are
asked to evaluate
their behavior in
terms of how
satisfied they are
with it and, more
importantly, in what
ways they would like
to be behaving that
are different from
what they are
observing.

1. To provide each
member with useful
feedback in regard to
how the person
currently relates in
the group.

2. Specific behavioral
goals are developed

2. To assist group
participants in

Activities

within the workshop setting by answering questions on behavioral change goal-setting worksheet and role-playing goal setting. Focus is on individual goal setting utilizing the following process: members form into two groups and complete Item No. 5 of the worksheet together. A group leader is present in each of these groups and aids in refining goals. On a separate sheet of paper, each member then writes out one selected target behavior and agrees to work on it in the following workshop sessions. Discussion should center around behavioral change goal inside the group. Focus in last sessions is on behavioral change goal outside the

Objectives

clarifying and setting specific behavioral goals.

Activities	*Objectives*

group, using the
feedback model for
their perception of
an appropriate
behavioral change.

3. Explanation of the
mini-group concept.
The emphasis in the
mini-group is on
expanding the
opportunity to
practice good
communications
outside the formal
group meetings and
to experience a
deepening
relationship with
selected others
through the use of
self-disclosure and
good feedback. The
need to bridge the
gap between what
takes place within the
formal workshop
setting and the real
world should also be
dealt with in relation
to the mini-group
experience.
Confidentiality of
mini-group
interaction as
separated from the

3. To introduce and
define the purpose
and activities involved
in the mini-groups.

Activities	*Objectives*

large group is
stressed.
4. Forming
mini-groups.
  a. Assigning
     members.
  b. Getting
     acquainted.
  c. Establishing a
     meeting time
     (exchange of
     names and
     phone numbers).
  d. Distribution of
     Exercise No. 1,
     not to be
     opened until
     group meets.
     (To help insure
     the trust level in
     the mini-group,
     the use of all
     mood-altering
     agents should be
     avoided.)
5. Material needed:
  1. Mini-group
     encounter
     booklets.
  2. Videotape deck,
     tape, and
     monitor.
  3. Pencils and
     paper.

SESSION 4

Activities	*Objectives*
1. Behavioral change goal sharing. After receiving behavioral change goal-setting worksheets, group members share their behavioral change goals with the other members of the group. Feedback is given with respect to the goal, and leaders explain that there will be peer ratings of progress toward goals.	1. To provide incentive for establishing constructive goals, an opportunity for feedback and assessment of goals, and modeling for others in the group as each group member shares his/her behavioral change goal with the group. Feedback can be given with respect to the goal. Leaders explain that there will be peer ratings of progress toward goals.
2. Mini-group sharing. This is a topic-focused discussion about the value of the mini-group experience in terms of behavior change goal setting, feedback, and other issues. Use of fishbowl technique may be helpful here.	2. To encourage mini-group activity; to provide an opportunity for group members to exchange information which might help all groups function more effectively.

Activities	*Objectives*
3. Positive feedback exercise. Each member asks the group for positive feedback, or "listen checks" can be used if desired. The group members giving the feedback call upon the others.	3. To aid group members in practicing the feedback model and to enable them to feel more relaxed in positive feedback.
4. Negative feedback exercise.	4. To provide members with the experience of giving and receiving information about behavior that is negatively perceived. Individuals are encouraged to tune in to this and deal with it in a constructive manner in an attempt to show that inter-personal anxiety-producing situations can be dealt with in nondefensive and personally rewarding ways. Using the "good feedback" model enhances the digesti-bility of the feedback and creates an atmos-phere which is more likely to result in its utilization.
a. Members sit in a circle with the person receiving feedback sitting in center or in opening of semicircle.	
b. Open feedback: people who wish to give negative feedback tell person in center what they wish to say (use "good feedback" model).	
c. Processing: after all persons in group have received neg-ative feedback, everyone dis-cusses how it	

	Activities		*Objectives*
	felt to receive such information. Stress is placed on the utilization of this input in their growth pattern.		
5.	Personal progress form. Using participants' worksheets to identify other participants' behavior change goals, each participant writes other participants' names on the outside of the blank slips of paper, his/her own rating of the other participants using a 1–5 scale, and also his/her own name on the inside of each slip of paper and places these slips in piles in the middle of the floor. Each participant will pick up his/her own slips, tally and average the scores and plot the number score on the graph located on the	5.	To provide each participant with concrete, peer-oriented feedback regarding progress toward goals.

Activities	*Objectives*
progress sheet. This will be done at the end of all remaining sessions, except the last session. The behavioral change goal–personal progress form is used here.	

SESSION 5

1.	Mini-group sharing. Open-group or fishbowl discussion technique is used to assess the value of the mini-group in helping achieve behavioral change goal and give useful feedback. Overall reaction to the mini-group concept is also discussed.	1.	To support and facilitate the impact of mini-groups on positive behavioral change as well as troubleshoot problems.
2.	Continue negative feedback exercise. The group members who did not participate last week sit in the center of the circle one at a time, or use the semicircle. The procedure followed	2.	Same as indicated for this exercise in Session 4.

Activities	*Objectives*
is same as reported in Session 4.	
3. Evaluation of behavioral change goal program. Same procedure as indicated in Session 4. Members are encouraged to discuss their feelings about their own progress and clarify any scores that confuse them. This method is used to facilitate their reaching their own goals and to give them another person's feedback.	3. Same as indicated for this exercise in Session 4.
4. "Outside the workshop" behavioral change goal setting (handout with discussion). The purpose of this activity is to enable each group member to establish a goal which he/she wishes to accomplish outside the group setting (i.e., in a dorm, in a class-room, with a	4. To help group members bridge the gap between the group setting and the real world.

Activities

friend, etc.).
Participants will have
had practice on this,
having worked on
their "in the group"
behavioral change
goal. Each member
receives a worksheet
for the out-of-group
goal setting and
spends time alone
working through
Item No. 4.

Objectives

SESSION 6

1. Mini-group sharing.
   General discussion.
   How did it go? How
   helpful was this
   session in
   comparison with
   previous ones? Are
   you working on your
   in-group behavioral
   change goal in the
   mini-group?

2. "Outside the
   Workshop"
   behavioral change
   goal setting (handout
   filled out to Item No.
   4). Members join
   their mini-groups to
   complete Item No. 5
   together. A group

1. Same as reported for
   this exercise in
   Session 5.

2. To help group
   members bridge the
   gap between the
   group setting and the
   real world; to provide
   opportunity to clarify
   behavioral change
   goals and overcome
   personal roadblocks.

Activities	*Objectives*
leader is present in each of these groups and aids in refining goals. Each member begins working on his/her goal as soon as possible. The mini-groups are to take time in their next two meetings to discuss each member's progress and/or problems concerning the goals.	
3. Continue negative feedback exercise. This activity is con- ducted as indicated in Session 4, except at the end the "group" (symbolically) goes to the center for feedback.	3. Same as indicated for this exercise in Session 4.
4. Personal progress form. This activity utilizes the same guidelines as in Session 4.	4. Same as indicated for this exercise in Session 4.

SESSION 7

1. Review of mini-group's final meeting and what the mini-group has	1. To assess the value and impact of the mini-groups for each participant as well as

Activities	*Objectives*
meant to participants.	determine the value of the mini-groups in the overall CSW.
2. Taking of post tests (if evaluation is being done). Rationale for testing done now is based upon the desire to receive both pre- and posttests for each participant prior to group's ending. Odds are better for accomplishing this goal during the last session than if a special testing time is scheduled for another date.	2. To evaluate the direction and amount of change that occurred as a result of participation in the CSW.
3. Debriefing regarding goals and group experiences. The remainder of this final session is oriented toward helping participants process feelings about their progress during the workshop.	3. To allow participants to process feelings about the progress they feel they have made on their own, "in" and "out of group" behavioral change goals, and to evaluate the effectiveness of the workshop.
4. Fantasy (15 min.). The group fantasizes a future hypothetical	

Activities   *Objectives*

meeting of the
group, e.g., at a
restaurant, at a party,
on a trip, at a social
get-together. The
group might also
fantasize how it
might help its
members further
their personal growth
in future meetings.

COUPLES ENRICHMENT WORKSHOP BY RICHARD BLOUCH.   The second communication skills group highlighted was developed by Richard Blouch at the Counseling Center at Millersville State College, Lancaster, Pennsylvania, and is entitled, "Couples Enrichment Workshop." It is designed to enhance normally functioning male-female relationships. It specifically excludes couples who are experiencing substantial conflict, or individuals whose relationship was so recently formed that expectations and roles have not had time to develop between partners. Blouch identifies five distinct purposes of the Couples Enrichment Workshop:

1. to assist couples to discover roles and expectations within the relationship;
2. to help partners discover the strengths and weaknesses of their relationship;
3. to help individuals discover the stereotypes and expectations which they have learned to project on their partners;
4. to increase openness and improve communications within the partnership; and
5. to reduce "gamesmanship" and increase authenticity and intimacy within the relationship.

Ideally, the number of participants should not exceed twelve. The workshop is designed to be offered in either two six-hour sessions, with up to a week intervening between sessions, or four three-hour sessions in consecutive weeks. Before the first session, the group leader conducts a screening interview with each couple seeking admission. Only couples who give evidence of a stable relationship should be selected. The motivation for wanting to be in the workshop must be to improve a relationship rather than to repair a relationship which is fraught with hostility, dominance–submission conflicts, or other disruptive patterns of relating. Another purpose of this interview is to select couples who are similar in regard to the length and nature of the relationship bond. A mixture of married, engaged, cohabiting, and dating couples can benefit from the workshop but not, in the opinion of the author, as well as a group of couples of similar relationship status.

The author provides an overview of the activities used and objectives realized during each of the four sessions of the Couples Enrichment Workshop. In order to use this outline for a two-session model, one simply combines the activities of the first two sessions into one six-hour session and does likewise for the last two sessions. The author clearly prefers the two six-hour session format because of the higher intensity generated within sessions and the increased continuity afforded. Below is the Couples Enrichment Workshop outline as developed by Blouch.

SESSION 1

Activity	Objective
1. Leader introduction (5 min.). Leader introduces self and the purpose of the workshop.	(1) To establish an open, trustful, atmosphere; (2) to encourage the exchange of perceptions by the partner; (3) to bring to awareness

Activities	*Objectives*
2. Introduction of workshop members via role reversal (20–30 min.). Partners introduce each other by assuming what they think are the characteristics of their mate.	the hidden agendas which partners have for their relationships.

3. Contracting by workshop members (20–30 min.). Each person writes at least one personal goal for the workshop. The goals are shared with the group and time is allowed for feedback.

4. Administration of the Barnett-Lennard Relationship Inventory, optional (30–40 min.).

5. Partnership roles (35–40 min.). Each participant makes a list of the roles he/she holds in his/her relationship and the roles held by the partner. Couples compare their lists. Agreement and

Activities   · *Objectives*

disagreement are
discussed within the
group.
6. Relationship
    sculpting (30–45
    min.). Partners take
    turns positioning
    themselves and their
    partners into human
    sculptures. The
    processing which
    follows relates to
    new learnings about
    the relationships and
    changes which
    couples would like to
    make.
7. Processing (variable).

SESSION 2

1. Male and female
    discussion groups
    (40–50 min.). Male
    and female groups
    meet separately to
    discuss what the
    opposite sex member
    of the partnership
    does which they like
    or are "turned-on"
    by. The groups
    report and discuss
    these appreciated
    behaviors. This

(1) To continue the open
exchange between partners
and couples; (2) to establish an .identity with the
workshop as a unit; (3) to
have couples learn about
and share the strengths and
weaknesses of their relationships.

Activities	*Objectives*
process is repeated for disliked behaviors.	
2. Dyadic interchange (45–60 min.). Couples take turns sitting in the middle of the circle for this exercise. The partners take turns telling each other five behaviors which they notice and emotions associated with these behaviors.	
3. Physical mirroring (20–30 min.). The participants are told to mirror their partner physically without any verbal communication. The subsequent group processing is aimed at discovering who leads and the ability to exchange and share leadership.	
4. Relationships Assessment Questionnaire (Peterman) is assigned as voluntary homework to be done before the	

Activities	*Objectives*
beginning of the third session.	
5. Processing reactions and feelings (variable).	

SESSION 3

1. Couples report on their use of the Relationship Assessment Questionnaire (20–30 min.).	(1) To help partners become sensitive to the verbally and nonverbally expressed needs of each other; (2) to teach and practice the helping skill of active listening (Gordon, 1970).
2. Echoing (25–40 min.). Starting with verbal mirroring or echoing, couples are taught Thomas Gordon's "active listening" skills. The group is broken into triads to practice this skill.	
3. Helping communications (60–75 min.).	
4. Nonverbal expression and recognition of emotions (15–20 min.).	
5. Processing (variable).	

SESSION 4

Activities	*Objectives*
1. Effective confrontation. Through the use of "I messages" partners learn how to tell each other negative effects they experience in their relationship without resorting to judgmental or guilt-inducing messages. "I messages" have a three part content: a. the emotion of the sender, b. the behavior of the partner, and c. the concrete effects of the partner's behavior on the sender (Gordon, 1970). 2. Problem solving for mutual satisfaction (45–60 min.). 3. Contract evaluation (20–30 min.). Participants check out the degree to	(1) To provide the participants with skills they can use in dealing with problems and conflicts in their relationships; (2) to help participants assess their learnings in the workshop; (3) to provide feedback to the leader which he/she can use in improving future workshops; and (4) to help participants experience a feeling of closure with the ending of the workshop.

Activities	*Objectives*

which their contracts
have been fulfilled.

4. The participants
   complete the
   sentence, "I learned
   that . . ." (30–40
   min.).

5. Leave taking (10–15
   min.). Each
   participant is asked
   to take leave of every
   other participant
   except his/her
   partner. This
   exercise provides
   closure for the
   workshop. I have
   changed this to have
   couples take leave of
   each other.

Decision-Making Skills Groups

A futuristic, changing society and an uncertain economy require individuals to know their options and to be able to make better decisions when faced with changes in life directions. Living in a complex, fast-paced society presents a person with multiple opportunities for involvement with the resulting need for making more decisions.

The ability to solve problems, choose among conflicting alternatives, and evaluate the quality of information are critical to effective functioning in our society. Individuals who have refined their skills in problem solving and in exercising reasoned judgment increase the likelihood that the decisions they make about future life directions will be fulfilling and satisfying.

DECISION-MAKING BY SI CLIFTON AND ROBERT NEJEDLO.   Decision-making skills groups usually consist of a series of exercises and talks which heighten people's awareness of the processes involved in arriving at sound decisions. The structured decision-making skills group described in this chapter, in some respects reflective of the Gelatt et al. materials developed by CEEB (1973), was developed by Si Clifton and Robert Nejedlo in the Student Development Center at Northern Illinois University, DeKalb. Their program is designed to make participants aware of the decision-making process, to consider alternatives, to predict outcomes, to develop strategies, and finally to make decisions based on a systematic process. A basic premise of the program is that the skills involved in decision making and the process utilized in arriving at a decision can be taught and practiced. The resultant learning can then be transferred to practical application in real-life situations.

Group Format. "Decision making" as designed by Clifton and Nejedlo has as its main purpose the providing of knowledge and skills which will help participants make better choices and consequently be able to enjoy more satisfying, productive life experiences. Group size is practically unlimited, and it has worked well with both small and large groups. Groups should have at least six members, and if more than twelve, one facilitator for each additional twelve should be added. There are three two-hour sessions. The format includes informative subject matter, decision-making activities, participant input, group interaction, informational handouts, and evaluation. A detailed description of the decision-making group as outlined by Clifton and Nejedlo follows:

SESSION 1 (two hours)

Activities	*Objectives*
1. Self-evaluation. Participants complete a self-evaluation from "Assessment of decision-making skills" (Handout No. 1) designed to determine the degree of their skill in making decisions.	1. To obtain a pretest measure of participants as decision makers.
2. Warm-up exercise. Group participants introduce themselves by using a "going-around" technique.	2. To begin to develop group cohesiveness.
3. Making decisions. Introduction to the decision-making process, the relative importance of decisions, and good vs. bad decisions through use of structured activities such as "Decisions come in all colors" (Handout No. 2) and "A good decision is . . ." (Handout No. 3).	3. To begin to understand the concept of decision making; to know that different decisions require different degrees of thought; and to understand what constitutes a good decision.
4. The person and the process in decision-making.	4. To understand the impact of one's values, use of

Activities	*Objectives*
Lecturette on major processes and limitations of skillful decision making.	adequate relevant information, and use of effective strategies; to understand limitations of personal capabilities, motivation, and environment.
5. Highlighting values. Discussion of one's personal values; recognition of one's own values and the values of others; use of exercises "A fantasy trip" (Handout No. 4) and "What do people really want" (Handout No. 5).	5. To begin to have one's own values and to respect the values of others.
6. Setting objectives. Establishing clear, concise objectives from one's values through use of exercise "Specifying what you want— objectives" (Handout No. 6).	6. To know how to formulate objectives that will let one know when the goal is attained.
7. Identify alternatives. Through use of a homework assignment, "What are your real alternatives" (Handout No. 7),	7. To enable the participants to learn the process of setting alternatives by establishing some real alternatives.

Activities	*Objectives*
participants are given a structured guide which takes them through the steps involved in establishing real alternatives. Each participant is asked to formulate alternatives to a given situation by stating objectives, obtaining further information, and accounting for abilities, interests, and values.	

SESSION 2 (two hours)

	Activities		*Objectives*
1.	Discovering your real alternatives. Lecturette on the process of identifying alternatives with opportunity for questions and discussion.	1.	To gain further insight into the process of identifying alternatives with the opportunity for integration into self.
2.	Using information in the decision-making process. Discussion of how to gain knowledge; and use of adequate, relevant information.	2.	To expand the participants' awareness of the importance of information.

Activities	*Objectives*
3. Information awareness. Discussion of how to gather information; the most common mistakes; and the consideration of sources, objectivity, and relevance.	3. To inform the participants of the value of critically analyzing input data.
4. Exercise, "Touch all bases" (Handout No. 8). An activity utilizing informational bases like people, reading material, audiovisual media, and computers. Participants are presented a case in which a student needs to decide whether or not he should remain in college. The group members are asked to brainstorm resources to be explored before making the decision.	4. To encourage discussion of additional sources of information without making judgment about which information is best.
5. Judging the quality of information. Criteria for evaluating information using	5. To enable participants to judge critically all information gathered.

Activities	*Objectives*
leader's expertise and exercise, "Do you believe what you hear and see?" (Handout No. 9). This exercise is intended to help participants discern information that is written to influence others from information that reports the facts.	
6. Predicting outcomes. This exercise consists of teaching and discussing the steps involved in predicting outcomes. The group leader assigns and introduces the "I predict" exercise (Handout No. 10). The exercise is a homework assignment presenting four situations which call for a decision. For each situation participants are asked to identify three alternatives and a predicted outcome for each alternative.	6. To acquaint the participants with the procedures in order that they will be able to do the take-home exercise.

SESSION 3 (two hours)

Activities	*Objectives*
1. Introduction. Discussion of the homework exercise and at the same time review of the steps in predicting outcomes.	1. To obtain feedback from participants relative to their involvement in the exercise.
2. Lecturette on risk taking. Discussion of the elements that influence the degree of risk people are willing to take and how to increase the chances of achieving a desired outcome.	2. To create insight regarding the range of risk-taking behavior.
3. Involvement in exercise "Shoot the works, play it safe, or ...?" (Handout No. 11). This exercise is designed to show that people differ in their risk-taking behavior and may not be consistent.	3. To learn one's own risk-taking characteristics as well as those of others.
4. Strategies for selecting alternatives. Discussion of types of strategies often used in selecting one alternative over another, such as desire strategy, success strategy,	4. To acquaint participants with various types of strategies so that they will be able to identify the strategies they utilize in making decisions.

Activities	*Objectives*
avoidance strategy and combination strategy.	
5. "X, Y, Z affair" (Handout No. 12). This exercise consists of making six decisions based on three alternatives. Additional information is provided after making each decision. The exercise allows a person to utilize a variety of strategies in making the six decisions.	5. To apply skills learned in the decision-making group; more specifically to know how to examine alternatives, use of strategies, preferences for probabilities, and desirability of outcomes in decision making.
6. Alternate exercise in decision making. If time permits, "Your agent" (Handout No. 13) can be used. In this exercise each participant is hired to make decisions based on certain information. A plan of action based on a strategy is to be written for each decision.	6. To gain further practice in decision making.
7. Summary: A review of the processes	7. To review and provide an

Activities	*Objectives*
utilized in good decision making.	opportunity for participants to clarify the decision-making process in order to integrate the knowledge.
8. Postevaluation. A postmeasure of decision-making skills is obtained through the use of the "Assessment of decision-making skills" self-evaluation form. This is the same form mentioned in Session 1.	8. To assess change and growth relative to knowledge of good decision making.

Career Planning Groups

Career planning groups attempt to help people discover ways to blend their life and work goals so as to increase their overall satisfaction with the direction of their lives. These groups are based on the assumption that people can distill from an inspection of their overall life experiences key elements that will help them create a meaningful life–work orientation.

Career planning groups have been variously labeled as Life Planning Workshops, Life Directions Workshops, Career Development Groups, PATH, and Career Decision-Making Groups. These approaches vary in the degree to which they focus on either establishing life directions or developing career objectives. For example, some life planning models might devote only one-fifth of the group time to actual consideration of career goals, while others might devote nearly the entire group experience to determining career objectives. Some life–work planning groups rely on external evaluation (ability tests or interest inventories) while others employ a self-assessment format.

PATH BY HOWARD FIGLER.   The career planning group highlighted in this chapter was developed by Howard Figler in the Counseling Center, Dickinson College, Carlisle, Pennsylvania, and is entitled PATH. According to Figler, the purpose of PATH is to provide a sequence of self-assessment exercises which assist individuals to create a life–work style that satisfies their internal and external needs. PATH operates on the premise that an individual can take charge of his/her life–work development only if he/she assesses all of the following factors: (1) the life priorities which will compete for attention with work priorities; (2) the chief values and pleasures that he/she hopes to satisfy in a life's work; (3) the abilities which he/she possesses and would most like to use in a life's work; and (4) a creative imagining of a situation in which all of his/her work needs might be satisfied and all of his/her talents might correspond to the needs of a particular work environment. Thus, the general objectives of PATH are to help the individual to:

1. integrate work priorities with life priorities;
2. find or create work situations in which he/she enjoys the work as much as possible;
3. choose work that he/she regards as highly important, worth doing, and intrinsically rewarding;
4. make use of his/her strongest talents, abilities, skills; and
5. create the idea of a life–work state in which his/her unique combination of values and talents is fully satisfied.

In order to achieve the stated objectives the PATH program has incorporated several key features. The key features identified by Figler are:

Self-assessment. The individual is the best judge of him/-herself; therefore, he/she makes all assessments of his/her personal attributes that are work related. No external assessment devices are used.

Client centered. Exercises serve as stimuli which enable individuals to intepret their own experiences; the student is given complete responsibility for these interpretations.

Group oriented. The sequence of exercises is designed for most effective use with small-group interaction. These exercises can also be used effectively in one-to-one counseling, or the individual can employ them on a self-instructional basis.

Option oriented. The program is chiefly helpful for those who have numerous options in their life–work planning, such as liberal arts students, and any other people who have the freedom to seek a wide variety of work possibilities.

Process oriented. PATH is not oriented toward decisions, closure, or final outcomes. Rather, it teaches individuals ways of thinking about life–work choices, and a process for sharpening their objectives. The process can be used by individuals again and again, whenever they desire to change objectives or a work situation.

Cumulative. PATH presents the view that everything an individual does in life can be applied to a future work situation. Since "nothing that you do is ever wasted," the individual has many degrees of freedom to experiment with work objectives.

GROUP FORMAT.   Selection of group members is not limited only to those who are undecided or unhappy over their career and life directions, expecially if that choice was based on a limited examination of a desired life style, underlying values, basic abilities, and functional skills. Since the PATH program requires approximately 15 hours of actual group time to complete, it is desirable that participants are prepared to invest the necessary amount of time and energy to make the process work. The number of participants can vary from as few as four to as many as thirty, with the ideal number being around twenty. The group format is designed so that approximately three exercises can be completed in each of the six, two and one-half hour sessions.

During the course of the sessions four major life–work dimensions are explored: (1) life–work style, (2) values, (3) abilities, and (4) creative career. Exploration in each of these four areas is accomplished by a series of exercises. Suggested time limits, format, and objectives as outlined by Figler are presented below. Many of the activities indicated below are described more fully in his publication titled PATH.

SESSION 1. Examining life–work style

Activities	Objectives	Format
1. Job style: "Security" "Excite-ment–risk" "Make money" "Free time" (45 min.)	1. To present individuals with four dramatically different motivations for working, and ask them to dwell upon the relative attractiveness for themselves.	1. Discussion in a small group of four following a brief talk by leader on characteristic differences among the four job styles.

Activities	Objectives	Format
2. Male/female: "How has your career development been affected by the sex role identification encouraged for you by significant others?" (45 min.)	2. To evaluate the influence of sex role identification upon an individual's life–work aspirations, and ask them to consider how these aspirations might have been different if they had been born the other sex.	2. Small group of four.
3. Distribution of time: "How do you choose to allot your time among (a) formal work, (b) informal work (off the job), and (c) recreation?" (60 min.)	3. To consider the relative importance of paid employment, nonpaid work, and leisure activity in terms of time individuals are willing to allocate to each.	3. Individuals work alone, then small group of four interacts.

SESSION 2. Exploring values

Activities	Objectives	Format
1. Life values vs. work values: "What conflicts may exist between your life values (family, community, geography, religion, health) and work values (money, power, security, fame, etc.)?" (60 min.)	1. To suggest that work needs must be compatible with other life priorities, if individuals expect to satisfy all life and work needs.	1. Individuals work alone, then interact with a group of four.
2. Traditional American values: "Which are the most important to you (health, happiness, stand up for rights, respect for	2. To explore values which are commonly espoused, and decide which of these the individuals regard as most important in their	2. Small group interaction.

Activities	*Objectives*	*Format*
parents, sick and needy, hard work and productivity, etc.)?"	life–work style.	
3. Work with people: "Which way of working with people is most appealing to you (instruct, supervise, negotiate, manage, counsel, etc.)?" (45 min.)	3. To ask individuals to discriminate among 15 different ways of working with people so that they may learn that some are much more appealing than others.	3. Small group interaction.

SESSION 3. Distilling key values

1. Occupational prestige: "Which occupations do not have enough prestige or status to satisfy you?" (30 min.)	1. To present individuals with titles of 90 occupations and ask them to discover their needs for occupational status by considering	1. Individuals work alone, then interact with a group of four.

Activities	Objectives	Format
	why certain titles would not be acceptable.	
2. Enjoyable activities: "What things do you most enjoy doing? How might you incorporate them into your future work?" (45 min.)	2. To discover the activities that are most purely pleasurable to individuals when they are freed from constraints by other people or organizations; to consider whether these preferences are compatible with the schooling or employment anticipated by the individuals.	2. Individuals work alone, then interact with a group of four.
3. Summary of values: "Review all of the values which you have determined from	3. To establish a unified record of all high priority needs and values identified by each individual.	3. Individuals work alone.

Activities	*Objectives*	*Format*
previous exercises; summarize these for use in the 'creative career' exercise later." (15 min.)		

SESSION 4. Examining abilities

1. Trial occupations: "Select six or more of these occupational titles which appeal to you. What might they have in common?" (A new "occupa-tional deck" of 150 cards is used here; 30 min.)	1. To introduce individuals to a wide array of occupations most often desired by college graduates, ask them to choose several on the basis of pure appeal, and then analyze the personal and subjective meaning that these choices may have for them.	1. Individuals work alone, then interact with a group of four.

Activities	Objectives	Format
2. Self-assessed abilities: "Rate yourself on these 30 separate abilities scales." (15 min.)	2. To obtain baseline data regarding individuals' assessment of their strengths and weaknesses, in terms of a set of general abilities that have direct relevance to a variety of occupations.	2. Individuals work alone.
3. Trial occupations and abilities: "Decide, with the help of your small group, which abilities are most essential to success in certain occupa-tions." (45 min.)	3. To examine certain kinds of work and discover what particular abilities are necessary for competence in these work situations; then, to evaluate the degree to which individ-uals possess the requisite abilities for the kinds of work that interest them most.	3. Small group interaction.

Activities	*Objectives*	*Format*
4. Functional skills: "Self-inventory your 'functional skills' from a roster of 85 such skills (managing, speaking, writing, computing, counseling, organizing, planning, building, etc.); then refer to experiences in which you have used these skills." (45 min.)	4. To have individuals consider which functions they perform best in work situations, and ask them to validate their view of these things they can 'do' by describing situations in which they have done them pre-viously.	4. Individuals work alone, then interact with a group of four.

SESSION 5. Identifying skills and creating career flexibility

1. Achieve-ments: "Name as many things as you can that you have done that (a) you	1. To examine the peak experiences of individuals for the discovery of hidden	1. Individuals work alone, then small group interaction, then "group interview"

Activities	*Objectives*	*Format*
enjoyed, (b) you did very successfully by your own standards, (c) you felt were important. Ask your small group to help you identify which functional skills you were using. Apply for a hypothetical job and talk about your skills." (75 min.)	talents; to ask individuals to talk about these talents in a situation where they might be applied to the needs of an employer.	for a hypothetical job.
2. Summary of abilities: "Review all of the abilities and skills which you determined from previous exercises and summarize these for use in the	2. To establish a unified record of all high-priority strengths that have been identified by individuals in cooperation with group members.	2. Individuals work alone.

Activities	*Objectives*	*Format*
'creative career' exercise later." (15 min.)		
3. Types of employers: "Self-inventory five or more kinds of or-ganizations which you would most prefer, from a roster of 80 employ-ers." (30 min.)	3. To ask individuals to begin thinking about the kinds of work environments that might best satisfy their personal needs.	3. Individuals work alone.
4. Random career: The group facilitator demonstrates that any combination of values, abilities, major fields, and employers can be integrated to form a sensible career;	4. To show that any com-bination of personal needs and attributes can be unified in a particular kind of work, if the individual applies some imagination to this process; to show that certain work	4. Facilitator demonstrates to the group and asks for their help in the process.

Activities	*Objectives*	*Format*
he/she does this by taking various values, abilities, fields, and employers from different group participants, and then creating a definition of an integrated career. (30 min.)	needs must not nec- essarily be surrendered in favor of other needs.	

SESSION 6. Creating career directions and evaluating options

1. Creative career: "Summarize your values, skills, preferred employers, and major field(s). Choose one employer you prefer, and decide	1. To construct the idea of a life's work which would incorporate all of an individual's highest priority needs, abilities, and other preferences.	1. Individuals work alone, then with assistance of small group of four.

Activities	Objectives	Format
how working for this employer might enable you to satisfy all of your personal attributes." (90 min.)	It best if this creative career is one which doesn't yet exist in the form defined by the individual.	
2. Group interview: "Report your 'creative career' to a small group of friends whom you haven't seen in years." (30 min.)	2. To provide the individual with practice in describing life–work aspirations, explaining them to people who may not understand readily, and interpreting how they fit his/her personal needs and attributes.	2. Small group members role play the "group of friends" and stimulate the individual to support and defend the career idea she/he has created.
3. Evaluation table: "Review your state of 'readiness' for career exploration	3. To deter- mine whether individuals have done the necessary investigation to support	3. Individuals work alone, then interact with small group.

Activities	Objectives	Format
by asking yourself relevant questions (Have I met people who do this kind of work? Do I know where the training is available? Do I know what resources are required?)." (30 min.)	their tentative life–work aspirations; to learn whether they have collected enough information to warrant an investment of time, resources, and energy toward this objective.	

Interpersonal Skills Groups

The ability to initiate, develop, and nurture meaningful interpersonal friendships can have profound effects on a person's sense of well-being and mental health. Many people, however, are unable to relate openly and comfortably with others. Those of us who work in mental health professions deal constantly with individuals who have been unable to initiate or sustain contacts with others or are unable to respond appropriately to people who reach out to them. In short, we work with many people who have not been successful in acquiring the interpersonal skills they need to nourish and improve their self-image.

During the past few years a number of structured groups have been designed to enable people to develop effective social and interpersonal skills. The goal of many of these programs is not only to increase participants' communicative skills but also to help them develop contact skills and create meaningful friendships. This is both a quantitative and qualitative goal. It is quantitative in that the programs try to help individuals increase the frequency of their interpersonal risk taking and social contact approach behaviors. By the same token the goal is qualitative in that the groups do not promote "interaction without integrity," nor do they consider increased frequency of interpersonal behavior a successful outcome unless some corresponding decrease in social anxiety and negative self-evaluative thinking has occurred.

The leaders of groups that focus on increasing an individual's ability to initiate and develop relationships must use extreme caution in their choice of exercises or procedures used during the beginning sessions. Participants often enter the group with a high level of anxiety that, if magnified by the initial activities, can become so inhibiting that some members will choose not to continue. Therefore, the first session at least should not be too demanding interpersonally and should be designed to reduce the counterproductive fear level evidenced by many participants.

FRIENDSHIP INITIATION AND DEVELOPMENT BY MICHAEL MENEFEE.
The interpersonal skills group described here is entitled "Friendship Initiation and Development," and was designed by Michael Menefee in the Counseling and Psychological Services Center at the University of Texas, Austin.

Before the beginning of the six two-hour sessions screening interviews take place. The purpose of the screening interviews is: (1) to obtain a commitment from each person to attend every session; (2) to screen out clients for whom the group may be inappropriate; and (3) to attempt to make the group heterogeneous with regard to degree of cautiousness in verbal expression. Ideally, the number of group members should not exceed twelve, including the two leaders. Below is an outline of the group as developed by Menefee.

SESSION 1

Activities	*Objectives*
1. Introductions (5 min.). Leaders introduce themselves, giving name and brief information about themselves. Then a name-chain game is used to introduce participants. One member is asked to introduce him/herself (as well as everyone to whom he/she has already been introduced) to person on his/her right, leaving the last person to recite the first names of all of the other members to the first person who started the chain.	1. To "imprint" members' names on each group member, as well as to establish a warm, friendly atmosphere.
2. Review of group format (5 min.). Leaders briefly discuss the goals of the program, emphasizing the	2. To clarify group structure roles and expectations of participants (especially in terms of providing content for

	Activities		*Objectives*
	focus on skill acquisition through modeling and behavioral rehearsal and on practice and performance of skills between sessions. Sessions usually consist both of set exercises and discussion of individual members' problems or concerns in the area of friendship development.		discussion and rehearsal of individual members' difficulties).
3.	Participant sharing of goals (45 min.). Leaders ask participants to tell the group why they came to the group, what their goals are in terms of coming to the group, and what their concerns are in friendship initiation and development. Leaders attempt to draw members out, specifically in terms of goals and member assessment of friendship difficulties.	3.	To emphasize importance of establishing goals for this experience, particularly in terms of changes each member hopes to realize within his/her own behavior.

Activities	*Objectives*
4. Modeling and rehearsal of initiating conversations (35 min.). Leaders introduce this exercise by commenting that the first three sessions will focus on skills involved in initiating conversations. Leaders briefly discuss these skills (asking open questions, providing and responding to "free personal information," and searching for an integrating topic of conversation). Leaders then model for several minutes an attempt to initiate conversation, demonstrating the appropriate skills. Members are then asked to form pairs and share and elicit basic but personal information about one another, attempting to ask open questions,	4. To begin to model and rehearse several of the more important skills in friendship initiation.

Activities	*Objectives*
respond to and provide unsolicited personal information or feelings, and arrive at a mutually interesting topic of conversation, if at all possible.	
5. Processing of exercise (15–20 min.). Leaders initiate a discussion of the participant response to and experience during the exercise, focusing on whether the conversation was balanced or shared, whether the content was relatively impersonal or personal, how the participant felt during the conversation (with attention to any positive or negative self-statements), and how the participant experienced his/her partner.	5. To review amount of success or difficulty encountered in the exercise; to encourage process of reviewing interactions and providing feedback to one another.
6. Discussion of homework (5 min.). Members are asked	6. To obtain base-line data.

Activities	*Objectives*
to monitor the frequency of initiated social approaches during the coming week using a monitoring booklet.	
7. Completion of feedback cards (5 min.). Members are asked to complete a session evaluation card.	7. To obtain session evaluation data.
8. Handout on "Initiating relationships."	8. To provide a cognitive framework of social approach.

SESSION 2

1. Collection and review of self-monitoring data (15–20 min.). Leaders collect self-monitoring booklets and inquire of participants what they learned, if anything, from monitoring, i.e., in what situations, if any, were they more likely to approach someone, what was ratio of initiated versus received	1. To obtain base-line data and to sensitize members to frequency and situational aspects of their approach behavior.

Activities	*Objectives*
approaches. Leaders emphasize situational aspects and individual variances; they also attempt to elicit negative and positive self-statements regarding specific successful or unsuccessful approaches. Risk taking is reinforced.	
2. Discussion of handout (15 min.). Leaders develop a discussion of handout distributed in Session 1, focusing on identifying facilitators, helpful "openers," and respondent cues suggesting interest in continuing the conversation.	2. To further develop cognitive framework, as well as define terms and desirable behaviors.
3. Continued practice in greetings and initial approach (60–75 min.).	3. To model and shape desirable behaviors of initial social approach.
a. Leaders ask several pairs of participants to model various	

Activities	*Objectives*
initial social approach situations (meeting someone in class, in the dorm, etc.). The situations may be elicited from the group or taken from the "Greetings and initial approach" cards (a deck of cards identifying situations and roles for two interactants for each situation). One partner of each pair is asked to attempt to initiate a conversation with his partner following role-play situational context. Emphasis is placed on sharing and eliciting personal information	

Activities	*Objectives*
(shifting from impersonal "What's your major . . ." to more personal "How do you feel about . . ." questions and statements), with continued reminders regarding asking open questions, providing "free information," and searching for an integrating topic. Each role play is processed on these dimensions. Repeat role plays until satisfactory models are shaped.	
b. After the basic skills have been modeled and clarified for and by the group, leaders distribute the "Greeting and	

	Objectives
Activities	
initial approach"	
cards to triads of	
group members.	
In each triad,	
the cards	
identify one	
observer and	
two interactants.	
All triads	
simultaneously	
practice role	
playing the	
desired	
behaviors, with	
the observer	
providing	
feedback to	
interactants at	
the end. Then	
participants	
change roles and	
repeat either the	
same situation	
or a new one	
(exchanging	
cards among	
triads.).	
c. Leaders develop	
a brief	
discussion of	
alternative	
hypotheses to	
personal	
rejection, should	
a social	
approach be	

Activities   *Objectives*

rejected or
terminated.
Participants are
encouraged to
consider various
reasons that
might cause
rejection other
than that one
might be
disliked, such as
the other might
not be "open"
to any more
relationships, or
that a "good fit"
between the two
was not present.
The develop-
ment of a
social network is
described as
involving sorting
out people you
enjoy and who
enjoy you, which
implies that
others may sort
one out as well.
To be "screened
out" is not,
however, to be
disliked.

4. Handout: "Example   4. To instigate behavior
    of homework   change outside the
    objectives," and   group.

Activities	*Objectives*

"Identification of homework objectives" (15 min.). Leaders distribute handout on typical objectives, focusing on the objectives listed under "initial approach" (versus repeated contact, spread, and arranging a future interaction). Leaders urge participants to select or create an objective that will extend and challenge their present level of skill or comfort, suggesting that different members will vary in what they consider difficult or important.

5. Distribution and collection of feedback cards (5 min.).

SESSION 3

1. Homework review (35 min.). Participants report on progress made	1. To reinforce and/or solve the problem on homework objectives in order to promote

Activities

toward the objective chosen last session. Leaders encourage group to: (a) help in problem-solving difficulties; (b) cognitively restructure harmful self-statements; and (c) elicit affective responses from members ("How did you feel when . . .?").

2. Exercise in self-disclosure (60 min.).

    a. Didactic. Leaders talk for a few minutes to and with the group about the process and reciprocal character of self-disclosure—how it is dependent on mutual sharing —and that pacing (distributing personal information over time) is extremely

Objectives

behavior change and risk taking.

2. To shape more open sharing of personal feelings and experiences; to desensitize participants who are anxious about self-disclosure.

Activities	*Objectives*
important as it allows interactants time to evaluate their interest in continuing the relationship. Appropriate self-disclosure, assuming neither participant terminates the process, develops trust and provides the conditions for a wide range of intimate behaviors. Leaders attempt to create a group discussion on this topic, noting that self-disclosure does not mean being completely honest or "telling all" the first time you meet someone (differentiating it from encounter group norms).	

Activities	*Objectives*
b. Leaders process this exercise with the group, focusing on determining which questions were perceived as most difficult, what level of disclosure was reached, and whether a feeling of closeness was engendered. Leaders reemphasize that disclosure is a critical but gradual process that produces trust and results from the decision to deepen a relationship.	
3. Discussion of Johari window (15 min.). A diagram of the Johari window is distributed and discussed.	3. To provide cognitive framework for self-disclosure.
4. Determination of homework objectives (15 min.).	

SESSION 4

Activities	Objectives
1. Review of homework objectives (25–30 min.). In addition to the usual procedure of reviewing homework experience, leaders attempt to elicit "feeling" talk, personal concerns related to homework or other events in relationship building.	1. To reinforce risk taking and performance of objectives, solve problems, and promote self-disclosure (more open responses to "How are you?").
2. Behavioral rehearsal of positive responses to individual participant concerns, skill or performance deficits (90 min.).	2. To individualize treatment of skill or performance deficits specific to each member. Furthermore, to provide additional practice in self-disclosure.
a. Leaders pass out blank cards to participants asking each to write down on a card a behavioral situation or interaction of concern or difficulty to him/her in area of friendship	

Activities	*Objectives*

      initiation and development (e.g., how to tell someone you don't want to get romantically involved; how to ask someone out for a date).

  b. Each person's specific concern or behavioral difficulty is discussed or role played in the center of the group, with focus on developing appropriate responses to the stressful situation. Leaders attempt to solicit and reactions from the group.

3. Identification of homework objectives (5 min.).

4. Completion of feedback cards (5 min.).

SESSION 5

Activities	Objectives
1. Review of homework objectives (35 min.).	
2. Coached modeling of appropriately providing negative feedback and disagreement (30 min.).	2. To demonstrate appropriate feedback and disagreement styles.
a. Group members role play providing criticism to a friend, with appropriate coaching on importance of specifying problematic behavior to the other, suggesting positive alternatives, conveying sense of continued interest in the relationship ("When you do X, I feel Y.").	
b. Group members role play disagreement, e.g., one partner voices an	

Activities

Objectives

opinion on a movie, other disagrees. Point out importance of forming your opinion as your personal reaction ("*I* was really moved by . . .") as opposed to making blanket, rigid statements ("That movie is bad and everyone should think so.").

3. Self-disclosure, providing feedback and personal reactions to one another (55 min.). Leaders ask participants to express one positive and one negative reaction to at least one other member's behavior, using appropriate feedback model. It is helpful to pull the group into a tight circle for this exercise. This

3. To provide information to participants regarding appropriate (likeable) and inappropriate (disturbing or distancing) behavior; to provide practice in providing and receiving personal feedback.

Activities	*Objectives*
experience should be introduced as an opportunity to learn about one's behavior and others' reactions to it. Leaders should attempt to clarify feedback, attending to recipients' emotional response.	
4. Identification of homework objectives (5 min.). Simply suggest members identify an objective, allowing a few moments for decision.	
5. Completion of feedback cards (5 min.).	

SESSION 6

1. Review of homework (25 min.).	
2. Personal feedback continued (50 min.). Ask group to form pairs and spend 5–10 min. sharing with each other their initial impression of each other, and how	2. To further provide specific information to each individual of his/her behavior and feelings as perceived by others; to provide warmth and closeness (usual result) through

Activities	*Objectives*
that impression has changed. Have members rotate to new partners and repeat this exchange. Leaders participate, providing any feedback they feel is appropriate (this is an opportunity to communicate privately with any specific individual in the group). Continue rotation until time is up or all possible pairs have exchanged impressions.	mutual disclosure of reactions.
3. Articulation of future goals and objectives (30 min.). Participants are asked to identify several behaviors they would like to change, increase, or decrease in frequency. Areas of change since group began are also discussed.	3. To stimulate members to consider developing personal change goals.
4. Distribution of Self-Monitoring booklets (5 min.). Leaders provide	

Activities	*Objectives*
same instructions as in Session 1, asking for the booklets to be dropped off or mailed at end of one week.	
5. Distribution of End-of-group evaluation Questionnaire (5 min.).	5. To obtain client satisfaction data.

Parenting Skills Groups

Being a parent is one of an individual's most important roles during his/her lifetime. Parenting can be a source of immense pleasure and reward as well as the cause of inner turmoil and feelings of inadequacy. It is little wonder that the nature of the "ideal" relationship between parents and their children has been the subject of numerous books and articles.

Increasingly people are becoming aware of the importance of developing effective parenting skills and are buying books and enrolling in programs to increase such skills. Within recent years several structured group models for developing key parenting skills have emerged and are gaining popularity. These models blend experiential activities, lecturettes, and homework assignments into a time-limited group format. To help insure the acquisition of effective parenting skills, homework assignments give parents a chance to reality test and implement the concepts and behaviors stressed during group sessions. Leaders often suggest that participants read one or more of the following books: *Between Parent and Child* (Ginott, 1965), *Parent Effectiveness Training* (Gordon, 1970), or *Living with Children* (Patterson & Gullion, 1971).

MORE EFFECTIVE PARENTING PROGRAM BY LESTER PEARLSTEIN AND JOEL LIPSON.   The parenting skills group described here is entitled "More Effective Parenting Program," and was developed by Lester Pearlstein and Joel Lipson in the Counseling and Psychological Services Center at the University of Texas, Austin. They indicate that in order to implement the model successfully, a leader should know the principles of behavior modification and have a general knowledge of basic helping skills and "good communication skills," as well as some knowledge of child development.

GROUP FORMAT.   The More Effective Parenting Program (MEPP) is designed for a group of approximately ten parents. Each of the nine weekly sessions lasts for 2 hours and is structured so that key parenting skills are developed in a carefully designed sequence. Because the skills acquired or accentuated during this program build on one another, then, it is detrimental to the program to leave out any of its components. The model is designed to be cofacilitated, and the time limits suggested for each activity should be viewed as guidelines and not as rigid determinants of activity length.

An overview of the group format, exercises used, and objectives sought for each session, as outlined by Pearlstein and Lipson, is presented below.

SESSION 1

Activity	*Objectives*
1. Introduction to structure and	(1) To Orient parents to structure, mechanics and

Activities	*Objectives*
mechanics of program—need for consistent attendance and starting on time (15 min.).	philosophy of MEEP program; (2) to sensitize parent to his/her implicit expectations from his/her children, and how these expectations might interfere with responsiveness to the child and creation of an atmosphere conducive to the emotional adjustment of the child.

2. Introduction of group members and use of some "ice breaker" getting-acquainted exercise. (15 min.).
3. Didactic presentation and discussion (15 min.).
   a. Home atmosphere conducive to optimal emotional development.
   b. "Love and limits."
   c. Importance of understanding, warmth, acceptance, guidance and support (use of employment and marital relation-

Activities	*Objectives*
ships as examples).	

4. Discussion of how home atmosphere is affected by parent's explicit and implicit expectations (15 min.).

5. Expectations exercise. (20 min.).
   a. Parent writes down kind of child he/she would like to have—descriptive adjectives.
   b. Parent writes down way child actually is—descriptive adjectives.
   c. Discussion of differences between "a" and "b"; expectations tied to "a" affect home atmosphere, parent's understanding, warmth, and acceptance.

6. Childhood memories exercise (20 min.).

Activities	*Objectives*

a. Parent is relaxed and comfortable.
b. List of common childhood experiences is read to help parent remember what it is like to be a child.
c. Brief discussion.

7. Didactic presentation and discussion of concept of script (25 min.).
   a. "What was your parent's script for you?"
   b. "How did this affect the atmosphere in your home?"
   c. "What is your script for your child?"
   d. "How might your script get in the way of your under-standing and acceptance?"

8. Homework assignments:
   a. List of stimulus situations.
   b. Parent asked to

Activities   *Objectives*

respond to "My
child would be
feeling . . ."
c. Parent asked to
attend to his/her
interactions with
child, and
identify own
feelings and
child's feelings.

SESSION 2

1. General discussion of homework (10 min.).
2. Competency exercise (20 min.).
   a. Each parent, in turn, labels feelings in one homework stimulus situation.
   b. Leader facilitates identification and labeling of feelings.
   c. Distinction made between feelings and overt actions.
3. Didactic presentation and discussion of the ways of communicating acceptance—

(1) To sensitize parent to child's feelings; (2) to sensitize parent to what he/she may be communicating to the child nonverbally; (3) to have parent become aware of and practice empathic

Activities	*Objectives*

nonverbally and
verbally (25 min.).
  a. Empty-chair
     exercise. One
     parent talks to
     empty chair and
     experiences what
     it feels like not
     to be responded
     to. Identify what
     leader could do
     nonverbally to
     make speaker
     more
     comfortable.
  b. Parent–child
     exercise. Parents
     form pairs and
     take turns
     playing child
     and parent.
     Child gets down
     on knees and
     looks up to
     standing parent
     and asks for
     permission to do
     something.
     Parent refuses
     firmly. Reverse
     roles.
  c. Brief discussion.
4. Didactic presentation
   and discussion of
   verbal communi-

	Activities	*Objectives*
	cation of acceptance and understanding—miscommunication vs. active empathic communication (10 min.).	
5.	Practice of empathic communication—messages broken into content and affect. Each parent in turn practices four ways of responding to message of another parent (50 min.).	
	a. Parroting response—word for word repetition.	
	b. Paraphrase content response —in own words.	
	c. Labeling of implied or expressed feeling.	
	d. Putting it all together. Responds in concise own words to content and affect (tone of voice important).	

Activities	*Objectives*

6. Homework
   assignments (5 min.).
   a. List of stimulus
      child statements.
      parent is asked
      to write
      empathic
      responses to the
      statements.
   b. Parent asked to
      list five
      statements by
      child during
      week, and
      empathic
      responses made,
      or empathic
      responses
      he/she would
      like to have
      made.

SESSION 3

1. General discussion of homework (10 min.).	(1) To increase understanding and comfort regarding use of empathic listening; (2) to expose parents to nonthreatening ways to express their own needs and feelings.
2. Competency exercise (40 min.).	
a. Parent asked to write down two	

Activities	*Objectives*

interactions with his/her child wherein feelings are implicitly or explicitly expressed.

b. Each parent, in turn, role plays one of these situations, delivering message to parent next to him/her.

c. Receiving parent responds empathically, and rest of group is encouraged to facilitate.

3. Didactic presentation and discussion of sequential order of parenting responses (10 min.). When empathic responding does not alleviate problem or satisfy parent's needs, parent may want to communicate own feelings and needs.

4. "You messages" as accusatory,

168   STRUCTURED GROUPS FOR FACILITATING DEVELOPMENT

Activities	*Objectives*
threatening communications of parent's feelings. "I messages" as clear statements of parent's feelings. Didactic presentation, modeling, discussion (10–15 min.).	

5. Practice of constructive "I" messages (40 minutes).
   a. List is provided of situations in which "I" messages would be appropriate.
   b. Each parent in turn responds to one of the stimulus situations using desctructive "You" message.
   c. Parent asked to identify potential consequences.
   d. Each parent, in turn, responds using "I" message.
6. Homework assignments (5 min.):

Activities

a. List of stimulus situations provided and parents asked to:
1. Respond using inappropriate "You" messages.
2. Identify potential consequence.
3. Respond using "I" message.
4. Comment on potential benefits.

b. Parent asked to generate five situations during week in which "I" messages were used or could have been used.

Objectives

SESSION 4

1. General review of homework (10 min.).

(1) To increase the parent's understanding and use of "I messages"; (2) to increase the parent's sensitivity to the reasonableness of his/her expectations; (3) to

Activities	*Objectives*
	enhance the parent's under-standing of and skill in set-ting rules or limits with his/her child.

2. Competency exercise (30 min.).
    a. Pick situation from previous week where "I" message was appropriate.
    b. Each parent, in turn, role plays or describes situation to next parent.
    c. Receiving parent asked to identify what his/her feeling might be and respond to an "I" message.
3. Discussion of relationship of response style and expectations. Importance of tolerance, flexibility, and checking out the reasonableness of expectations (10 min.).
4. Exercise: Reasonableness of expectations.

Activities

Worksheet gives
parent chance to
identify expectations,
tolerance limit,
child's real
capabilities and
difficulties—
discussion (25 min.).

5. Didactic presentation
   and discussion of
   limit setting as next
   phase in sequence of
   parent response (15
   min.).
   a. Review of
      guidelines of
      limit setting.
   b. Explanation of
      natural and
      logical
      consequences
      when limit is
      exceeded.

6. Practice in setting
   limits and making
   rules using
   guidelines (25 min.).
   a. From worksheet
      of exercise,
      reasonableness
      of expectations,
      parent is asked
      to select
      situation
      requiring limit.

Objectives

Activities   *Objectives*

   b. Leader models setting limit.
   c. Each parent, in turn, verbalizes rule or limit he/she would like to express to child, and appropriate consequence if limit is exceeded.

7. Homework assignments (5 min.). Generate five situations during week in which interaction with child calls for the expression of a rule or limit. Include expectations, limit to behavior actually tolerated, verbalized rule or limit, consequence, enforcement.

SESSION 5

1. General review of homework (10 min.).
2. Competency exercise (40 min.). Each parent in turn de-

(1) To increase understanding and use of consecutive limit setting; (2) expose parents to the prerequisite consideration for

Activities	*Objectives*

scribes a situation from his/her homework and how he/she responded to it.

increasing the frequency of occurrence of desirable child behaviors and decreasing the occurrence of less desirable child behaviors.

3. Discussion of sequence of parental responses leading to modification of child's behavior.
4. Didactic presentation in which parent is instructed in the following (30 min.):
   a. The importance of operationally defining behaviors to be modified.
   b. Observing and recording behaviors.
   c. Surveying reinforcers operating in the environment of the child.
5. Practice and discussion (35 min.).
   a. Operationally define and determine a method of measurement for the modification of

Activities	*Objectives*
representative behaviors.	

b. Generate lists of reinforcers specific to particular children of the participants.

6. Homework assignments (5 min.).:

a. Parent is asked to choose, define, and determine a practical method of measurement for each of two behaviors exhibited by his/her child.

b. Parent is asked to survey the reinforcers relevant for his/her own child.

SESSION 6

1. Homework and competency exercise (60 min.).	(1)To insure that parent has adequately defined and chosen an appropriate method of measurement for be-
a. Each parent, in	

Activities	*Objectives*
turn, shares with the group the behaviors chosen to be modified, and method of measurement selected.	haviors to be modified; (2) to insure that reinforcers chosen by the parents are practical and realistic; (3) to introduce parents to concept of baseline recording; (4) to introduce parents to a method for graphing data.

b. Each parent provides representative examples of the reinforcers chosen for use with his/her child.
c. Leader provides feedback concerning potential problems.
2. Didactic presentation and practice (50 min.).
   a. Emphasis on the importance of baseline recording.
   b. Instruction in base-line recording.
   c. Practice in graphing base-line data as it relates to the

Activities	*Objectives*
individual needs of the parents.	

3. Homework assignments (10 min.).
   a. Parent asked to begin base-line recording (and graphing) of at least one of the behaviors selected earlier.
   b. Parent asked to bring base-line graphs to next meeting.

SESSION 7

1. Homework and competency exercise (25 min.).

(1) To straighten out problems encountered during week in regard to baseline recording and graphing; (2) to introduce principles of behavior management; (3) to instruct in design of program of intervention.

2. Didactic presentation (40 min.). Introduction of general principles of behavior management (consequences, immediacy, and

Activities   *Objectives*

consistency in
providing
reinforcers).

3. Practice and
discussion (35 min.
for a. and b.; 20 min.
for c., d., and e.).
   a. Parent designs
   intervention
   program specific
   to child's
   behavior he/she
   wishes to
   change.
   b. Leader facilitates
   by working
   individually with
   parents.
   c. Parent shares
   intervention
   program with
   rest of group.
   d. Group members
   facilitate and
   provide
   feedback.
   e. Leader facilitates
   and moderates.
4. Homework
assignments (5 min.):
   a. Parent asked to
   implement
   program he/she
   just designed.
   b. Parent asked to

Activities	*Objectives*
continue day-by-day graphing for presentation at next session.	

SESSION 8

1.	Homework and competency exercise (85 min.).	(1) To provide opportunity for discussion of results of first week of intervention; (2) to provide opportunity for problem solving with parents whose interventions have provided minimal results.
	a. Each parent, in turn, exhibits and discusses graphic representation of child's behaviors.	
	b. Parents are encouraged to share frustrations and elations occurring during first week of intervention.	
	c. Leader and other members facilitate.	
2.	Didactic presentation (30 min.). Instruction in evaluating and changing own programs based on data collected.	

Activities

3. Homework assignments (5 min.):
    a. Parents asked to continue intervention program as well as the day-to-day graphing of child's behavior.
    b. Parent asked to bring the graphic presentations to final session.

SESSION 9

Activities

1. Homework and competency exercise (60 min.). Each parent, in turn, exhibits the graph of child's behavior, and explains graph and problems encountered.

2. Leader attempts to summarize and overview past seven sessions (15 min.).

3. Discussion and recommendations (45 min.).

Objectives

(1) To facilitate parent in reevaluating and making necessary changes in behavioral management programs; (2) to facilitate an integration of all of the skills and concepts presented during previous weeks.

Self-Management Groups

The elimination of self-defeating behavior and the development of self-managing capabilities have been the focus of much discussion in the field of human growth and development. Within the past few years more and more counselors and other mental health workers have been using approaches which encourage the development of self-management skills on the part of their clients. To some extent this radical increase in the utilization of such procedures has been the result of the publication of numerous articles and several informative books (Watson and Tharp, 1972; Cudney, 1975; Williams and Long, 1975) that provide counselors with a broad array of strategies for aiding client self-management.

Self-management groups have the twin goals of remediation and development. The remedial goal involves the elimination of some self-limiting behavior or problem. The developmental goal has to do with the development of an approach to life or strategy that enables persons to manage their lives so that they do not reacquire problem behaviors.

PROFILE GROUPS FOR WEIGHT CONTROL BY ROBERT B. MANDELL.
The group program chosen to exemplify this approach is entitled "Profile Groups for Weight Control," and was designed by Robert Mandell, Coordinator of Counseling and Health Services at the University of Texas, Dallas. As the title implies, this group is designed to center on one aspect of a person's behavior which can be self-controlled. Although the typical self-management group relies almost exclusively on a behavioral format, Mandell's approach combines behavioral principles and growth group techniques to resolve the problem and establish positive behaviors.
Group Format. The stated purpose of the group is to provide a structure and an atmosphere which can help people

lose excess weight and develop the skill to maintain their desired weight. The ideal number of group participants is ten, with six being the minimum and twelve being the maximum. Inclusion in the group is by self-selection. Each of the ten group sessions lasts approximately 90 minutes, except for the first meeting which focuses on organizational issues and usually lasts about one half-hour.

An overview of group format, exercises used, and objectives sought in each session as suggested by Mandell are presented below.

PRESESSION

Activities	*Objectives*
1. General introduction and organizational meeting (30 min.), designed to: (a) clarify the group purpose and procedures, including fact that initial weight of each group member and weekly progress toward stated goals will be known to all other group members; (b) establish a common meeting time and place.	(1) To insure a clear understanding of the group goals, responsibilities, and procedures; (2) to encourage only those who evidence some degree of seriousness and commitment to weight control to join the group.
2. Expectation by leader: (a) each member should be serious and	

Activities	*Objectives*
committed to goal; (b) public accountability will exist within the group.	

SESSION 1

1. Use nonthreatening group exercises designed to create closer interpersonal relationships such as those found in *A Handbook of Structured Experiences for Human Relations Training* (Vols. 1–4) by Pfeiffer and Jones. (30 min.)

   (1) To establish baseline weight and realistic end goal; (2) to establish a positive group atmosphere and group cohesiveness so that sharing of actual weight is nonthreatening and personal reinforcement value of each group member is increased.

2. Restate goals and negotiate group rules (30 min.).
   a. Group members and leader share in establishing group rules.
   b. Typically, rule discussions center on issues of attendance, confidentiality, and weight.
3. Establish base-line weight for each

	Activities	*Objectives*

group participant (10 min.).

a. Group members have to post weights on chart.

b. Shoes are removed before weight check.

4. Leader initiates discussion on goal setting, i.e., weight loss goal (20 min.).

a. Each group member's goal should be self-determined.

b. Group leader monitors goal setting to encourage establishment of realistic goal.

SESSION 2

1. Group begins with weigh in and posting of new weight. Calculate weight loss average for entire group. Reinforce those who made progress toward the goal (10 min.).

(1) To provide useful hints and ideas so that group members can develop effective self-management strategies; (2) to unlock some of the feelings and tensions which people have about their bodies and body image; (3) to continue to build

Activities

Objectives

up the personal reinforcement value of each group
member.

2. Leader facilitates a
discussion among
participants about
the type of
intragroup incentives
for weight control
that they wish to
build into the
process (25 min.).

3. Leader provides
informational
assistance on
weight-control
techniques and
encourages members
to do the same (20
min.).
   a. Supply articles
   and books on
   dieting and
   weight control
   (e.g., Handout
   "Scary Facts").
   b. Assign one of
   the handouts for
   reading.
   c. Point out
   differences in
   philosophies and
   techniques for
   weight control
   d. Leader may use
   Stillman's book,

Activities   *Objectives*

*The Doctor's Quick
Weight Loss Diet*
for developing a
list of practical
hints. Some
examples are:
(1) Break up
your meal. Put
aside what you
haven't eaten for
a snack later or
for the next day;
(2) Watch out
for common
rationalizations,
such as, "I'm
already 15
pounds
overweight, so I
decided what's
the difference if
I eat just a little
more."

  e. Discuss materials
and reactions.

4. Either through the
use of traditional
group counseling
methods or
sensitivity group
exercises begin the
process of
encouraging people
to share feelings
about their bodies,
self-images, or other

Activities   *Objectives*

life areas (30–40
min.).

SESSIONS 3–8

1. Group begins with
   weigh-in process as
   described earlier.
   Continue to
   reinforce individual
   progress and allow
   the group to
   encourage and
   support the less
   successful members
   (10 min.).
2. The group leader
   initiates a therapeutic
   sharing of feelings
   and experiences of
   the past week with
   regard to weight
   control. Once he/she
   initiates the group
   process the leader
   utilizes a
   client-centered frame
   of reference, relying
   on the mutual trust
   and cohesiveness of
   the group to
   stimulate the process
   of sharing feelings
   and attitudes about
   weight loss,

(1) To reinforce successes
in order to support cumulative gains; (2) to continue to
explore hopes and fears
about the body, self, and social interactions that affect
weight control; (3) to begin
to blend from group rein-
forcement of successes to a
focus on self-maintenance
skills; (4) to continue to foster a healthy group atmo-
sphere insuring that people
feel safe in examining sensitive interpersonal and intrapersonal feelings.

Activities   *Objectives*

maintenance of new
weight levels, and
experiences
participants have had
associated with
weight loss and
control.

3. Throughout these
sessions increasing
emphasis is placed
on techniques and
approaches designed
to help a person
maintain weight loss.
Weekly handouts and
discussions provide a
wide range of weight
control strategies
from which to
choose (20 min.).

SESSION 9

1. Group begins with
final weigh in using
established
procedures (10 min.).

2. Group discusses
feelings about goal
attainment or failure
to achieve goal (20
min.).

3. General sharing of
feelings and attitudes
about leaving group

(1) To help each group
member understand the factors leading to goal attainment or lack of it; (2) to
insure that each member
has developed an effective
self-management plan; (3)
to help members summarize
and clarify what they have
learned about themselves in
regard to weight control; (4)
to insure a smooth ter-

Activities

includes a discussion of the procedures that each member has chosen to maintain weight control. Encourage each group member to provide any helpful suggestions he/she can think of to others in the group (50 min.).

4. Solicit suggestions for improvement of group format (10 min.).

Objectives

mination of the group; (5) to obtain feedback for improvement of future groups.

SUMMARY

This chapter contained detailed descriptions of nine life skills groups that are either comprehensive in scope or have achieved fairly widespread use. Included with the program descriptions were the objectives for each session and the names and locations of the program developers. The next chapter will highlight six distinct types of life theme groups which focus on issues such as loneliness, intimacy, sexuality and self-esteem.

Chapter 4

LIFE THEME GROUPS

Whereas the goal of life skills groups is essentially to enhance *inter*personal functioning, life theme groups are designed to deal with vital *intra*personal issues. Seemingly
intangible, yet strongly felt needs essential to living a satisfying life and to setting and achieving personally meaningful goals are the focus of discussion in life theme groups.
In a very global sense, the objectives of these structured
groups are to clarify individual values and to help each
participant make an active, personal commitment to adopting or adapting a lifestyle that will be consistent with them.

FOCUS OF LIFE THEME GROUPS

Specific examples of themes commonly addressed in such
groups include sexuality, mortality, sharing oneself, loneliness, selfhood, intimacy, personal values, and the like. As
stated in Chapter 2, the inability to resolve these issues

satisfactorily for oneself can result in the living of an unexamined, purposeless, and unfulfilling life. The most common titles given to life theme groups would be similar to the following: "Intimacy," "Sexuality," "Loneliness and Self-Betrayal," "The Meaning of Death in Life," "Learning to Love," "Sharing and Relationship," "On Being a Man," "Women in Search of Autonomy," "Search for Fulfillment," "Clarifying Personal Values," "Self-Esteem," "Living Together," "Body Image," and "Self-Concept."

Life theme groups have some common characteristics, regardless of the specific thematic focus. These common aspects have been examined in detail in Chapter 2, but for the sake of clarity, the four are restated here.

1.   Each group has a clear purpose generally shared by all group members.
2.   Life theme groups focus primarily on intrapersonal understanding as opposed to the acquisition of interpersonal skills.
3.   By helping participants to increase their self-understanding, life theme groups help them become flexibly responsive, rather than rigid or role dependent.
4.   The format for each life theme group involves: (a) a series of structured exercises to facilitate the self-inquiry process, (b) techniques for integrating and resolving the particular theme focus, and (c) a predetermined meeting length or time structure.

Typically, the group leader coordinates the process and sequence throughout, but is less directive and less personally active than is the leader of a life skills group. Also, life theme groups involve less overall time investment, with most groups meeting formally for maximums of eight sessions and a total of 15 hours.

As can be seen from their titles, life theme groups, although fairly well structured, revolve around topics which are frequently existential or humanistic in nature. While careful preselection of participants is characteristic of most life skills groups, such screening is not so crucial to the success of a life theme group. However, it is important to acquaint participants with the distinction between group therapy and the structured life theme group experience in which they are about to participate. A final point of note may be somewhat obvious; that is, while many participants achieve major gains toward a satisfactory resolution of the focal issue, others find that the group experience represents merely the beginning of the crucial process of examining and valuing their particular position vis-à-vis the theme.

DESCRIPTION OF LIFE THEME GROUPS

The remainder of this chapter describes a number of life theme groups, chosen for inclusion because of their relative completeness, variety of focus, and developmental aspect. The descriptions are in narrative form in contrast with the outline style used for the more highly structured life skills groups.

Clarifying Personal Values by Judy Marsh

A basic human need for effective functioning is the clarification of personal values so that one can pursue a lifestyle in accordance with them. A model for resolution of this critical theme is that used by Judy Marsh, formerly of the Office of Residential Life at New England College, Henniker, New Hampshire. Her description of the workshop follows.

GROUP FORMAT.   Most of the decisions we make in life are based on how and why we value things. Yet, so often one hears people say, "I do not know why I do this," or, "I wonder why I always do that." The answer is probably linked to something they value—some need that is being met by that action.

Values clarification sessions can be useful for people of all ages and in all career positions. The number of people in a workshop is up to you as a facilitator, according to what size group you prefer. This particular program has been used with anywhere from 20 to 150 people in various workshops. Each session is designed to run from 45 to 90 minutes.

A primary goal is to have people get in touch with their own personal values. It is important to share the seven criteria for a full value at the beginning of the first session (Raths, Harmin, and Simon, 1966). A full value meets the following seven criteria:

1. chosen freely;
2. chosen from among alternatives;
3. chosen after due reflection;
4. prized and cherished;
5. publicly affirmed;
6. acted upon; and
7. part of a pattern that is a repeated action.

As you share the value criteria, choose a full value from your own life. Tell how you chose it, how you considered the alternatives, the time you spent reflecting on it, and so on, down the criteria list.

As facilitator, it is also important that you model what you ask others to do, particularly in the initial exercise. I use an extra large piece of newsprint or overhead projector and do each step as a model for them to see as they write on their own. This serves several purposes: it answers many of the directional questions; it gives you a better sense of timing for each phase; and it shows the group that you are working on your own values, and are willing to affirm them publicly.

The following six sessions have been drawn from several sources and together provide a total design which is quite useful in assisting people to clarify their personal values.

SESSION 1. Name tags (60–90 min.)

This exercise is an easy way to help any new group relax and get acquainted. It also starts individuals on the road to identifying what they value in their own lives, and to affirming those values in a group. You will need a sufficient number of 5X8 unlined file cards, pens, and safety pins.

Hand out the cards and have participants write their names or the name they would like to be called in the center of the card. Ask them to write the numbers 1 to 3 toward the upper right hand corner of the card, and then proceed with the following instructions. Title this section "favorites." Next to number 1, list your favorite song; for number 2, list your favorite way to spend Saturday night; and for number 3, list your favorite food.

Then, move to the bottom right hand corner and number 1 to 3 again. Title this section "places." For number 1, name what you feel was the warmest, most comfortable room in your house when you were age seven. For number 2, list what you feel is the warmest, most comfortable room in your present living space. Finally, for number 3, note your favorite vacation place.

Now move to the bottom left hand corner and number 1 to 3 again. This corner will be your "people" corner. For number 1, name the three most nourishing people in your life. These would be three people you like to be around most, and who really make you feel good about yourself. For number 2, indicate who is the most toxic person in your life. "Toxic" as used here means that the person you have identified is a drag to be around, does not appreciate you for who you are or what you do, and probably makes you feel not good about yourself. For number 3, write the name of the person in your life from whom you need more validation. This might be a person you see everyday or someone who is far away—but you need to hear from this person that you are "OK," and positive viewing of you by this person is important to you.

The last section in the upper left hand corner is the "me" section, the place for things about you. Again, write the numbers 1 to 3. Next to number 1, list three qualities you like about yourself. By number 2, put down one thing new you have done to make your life better this past year. It might be something you changed, like wearing seat belts or stopping smoking, but it should have had an influence that to you has improved your life. For number 3, write down one thing you could do to enrich your life more in the next six months.

After all participants have finished their cards, they pin them on themselves. For a few minutes they walk around silently and read each others' name tags. Then they form groups of three, sit down, and take turns sharing one item on their card—the item of their choice. They have two minutes each to do so. Then they have three more minutes each to share one of the areas in the "people" section.

For the last part, participants have two minutes each to share the three qualities about themselves that they like best. People continue to wear their name tags throughout the day since they serve as good conversation starters and they enable everyone to relate to one another by name.

SESSION 2. 20 Loves (45 min.)

This session is designed to put individuals in touch with the activities that nourish, energize, and relax them. It requires that each participant have a piece of paper and pencil or pen.

Instructions: Take a sheet of paper and write the numbers 1 to 20 in the center. To the right of the numbers, draw vertical lines that divide that half into seven columns. Now think of the things in your life you like to do most and list them on the left side of the numbers. These may be big or small things. The most important criterion is that *you* enjoy doing them.

1. Now in column 1 put an "A" next to those things you like to do alone. Put an "O" next to those things you like to do with others. Put an "A-O" next to those things you like to do alone as well as with others.

2. In column 2 put a dollar sign "$" for activities that cost you $5.00 or more every time you do them.

3. In column 3 draw a heart next to those activities you need or want to do with someone you love.

4. In column 4 put "52" next to those activities you would like to do once each week for the rest of your life.

5. In column 5 put an "E" next to all the activities that involve exercise.

6. In column 6 put "80" next to the activities you still will be able to do if you live to be eighty and are in good health.

7. In column 7 jot down the approximate date you last did each of these activities.

It is helpful here to have prepared a large sample sheet to give the participants a visual picture of how their sheet should appear.

Now divide the participants into groups of four and

complete the following sentences about their findings from this exercise:

What I learned was ....
What I relearned was ....
What I was surprised to see was ....
What I need to do is..........................

Give each group eight to ten minutes to do their group sharing. Then ask if people would share their findings with the group as you call on them.

Session 2 is modified from Simon (1974).

SESSION 3. The pie of life (45–60 min.)

All of us have at one time or another said, thought, or heard from others the phrase, "I don't know where my time goes!" This session helps people to realize where their time is going and how they are expending their energies. Each person will need a sheet of paper and a pencil or pen.

The facilitator begins by drawing a large circle on the board or on newsprint. Then the group is told that this circle represents a typical day in their lives. Divide the circle into quarters with dotted lines. Each quarter represents 6 hours. Now participants are to estimate how many hours or parts of an hour they spend on each of the following areas of activity in a typical day:

1. Sleep;
2. in classes (if group includes students);
3. at work (a job that earns money);
4. with friends, socializing, playing sports, etc.;
5. on homework or preparations for classes (again, if students present);
6. Alone, reading, listening to stereo, watching television;

7. on chores, laundry, housework, etc.;
8. with family, including meal times;
9. on miscellaneous other pastimes.

Participants draw with solid lines a proportional slice within their circle for each of the nine areas and label each slice. When everyone is finished, each person finds a partner. They ask themselves the following questions and share with their partners the answers to them:

1. Are you satisfied with the sizes of each area slice?
2. Ideally, how big would you want each slice to be? Draw your ideal pie.
3. Realistically, is there anything you can do to begin to change the size of some of your slices?
4. Is there something you would like to make as a "contract" with yourself to change?

This is what a self-contract is:

I _____(your name)_____ TO BETTER MY LIFE WILL

(whatever you need to do.)

_____Your signature.
_____Signature of a friend (witness).
_____Reminder date—friend calls up and reminds you of your contract.
_____Date contract is to be completed.
_____The date and way you and your friend will celebrate the completion and burning of your contract.

Session is borrowed from Simon, Howe, and Kirschen-baum (1972).

SESSION 4. Barometer of values (45–60 min.)

The purpose of this activity is to help people acquire insight into their own value positions and gain an awareness of the value systems of others. For this segment, it is suggested that you use a wide felt-tip marker and seven large sheets of paper, preferably newsprint. You will also need some tape. In this strategy it is necessary to identify and number specific locations around the room which may be done using paper and felt pens to designate the locations in sequence from –3, –2, –1, 0, 1, 2, 3. This scale is representative of the following:

-3   strongly disagree
-2   moderately disagree
-1   slightly disagree
 0   no feeling
 1   slightly agree
 2   moderately agree
 3   strongly agree

To start, have the whole group cluster at zero. Tell them you will read a value statement twice and then they should move to the specific location that best represents their feelings. Ask them to be aware of how they move, and how others move in response to their value posture on each statement. You may repeat the sentence if asked, but be sure that you do not modify the wording of the statements. Here are some sample value statements:

1.   Children under ten are responsible enough to make decisions.
2.   Premarital sex is okay.

3. People learn violence from spanking.
4. The father should have the final say-so in family decisions.
5. Women are more effective dealing with young children than men.
6. Children should be able to make up their own minds about attending church.
7. Grades children earn in school are entirely their own business.
8. Alcohol is a more dangerous drug than marijuana.
9. Masturbation is healthy and natural.
10. Pornographic materials should be kept out of the schools.
11. It is inappropriate for professional men to wear long hair.
12. A complete sex education course, including sexual methods, should be taught to teenagers in the schools.
13. Birth control pills and devices should be dispensed through the schools.
14. Formal education is the key to success in life.
15. People with strong, formal religious beliefs are most effective when dealing with young people.
16. Men who cry are weaker than men who don't.
17. I support the principles of the women's liberation movement.
18. Divorce laws should be stricter.
19. I support capital punishment for rapists.
20. Parents should be encouraged to stay together for the sake of the children.
21. There should be stricter abortion laws.

Now ask the group to find four or five individuals with whom they frequently shared similar positions during the exercise. After they have formed their group, repeat five of your value statements again. Have each group choose one statement for themselves. Then have them respond to the following questions surrounding that value statement:

1. How do you hold these values?
2. What is the source or origin of these values?
3. How do you act on these values?
4. What validating experiences have you had which affirm these values for you?

Session 4 has been adapted from a Parent Effectiveness Training (P.E.T.) course (Gordon, 1974), as taught by Bert Cohen.

SESSION 5. What would you like to say to the world?
(35–40 min.)

The purpose of this session is to focus on one important value and determine how one feels about it. Materials needed include a large pad of paper (18X24), crayons or colored markers, and tape.

Instructions: Each of you has been given a large piece of paper that is to represent a free billboard your town council has just given to you. It is located on the main street or highway of your town or city. You are to use that billboard to display any message you want to give to others. Compose that message in any way you see fit, in response to the question, "What would I like to say to the world?"

After all have finished their billboards, each member tapes his/hers up around the room. Then, volunteers identify their billboards and share their meanings and why they chose them. Not all billboards need to be described, but sufficient time should be allowed to have several different ones explained.

SESSION 6. Personal medallion (45–60 min.)

The objective for this session is to have individuals think about the direction and quality of their own lives. For this exercise, each person needs paper and a pen or marker of some type.

Begin by having participants draw a circle about 9 inches in diameter on their sheet of newsprint. In the center of that circle they draw another circle about four inches in diameter. Next, they draw a line from the outer circle to the inner circle at approximately the 1:30, 4:30, 7:30 and 10:30 positions on the outer circle, as if it were the face of a clock (see Fig. 1).

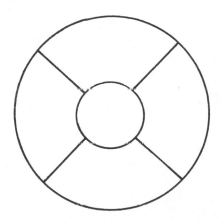

Figure 1

In the first section at the top of the "medallion" they symbolize what they would do if given a whole year to do anything they wanted with unlimited funds and guaranteed success. Going clockwise, in the next section they symbolize what in their lifetime they consider to have been their greatest personal achievement. In the bottom section, they symbolize three things they do to reenergize and relax. In the last section they symbolize one thing other people can do to make them happy. Finally, in the center circle, they symbolize three qualities they would like others to remember about them. All of these symbols preferably should be graphic, although they may be verbal if no visual symbol is feasible. When participants are finished, they divide into groups of three. In these groups individuals take turns explaining their medallions and the meaning of each symbol. This is the final session of the workshop, and it provides a personal summarizing activity which draws together the elements addressed in the previous five meetings.

Some additional factors are very important for a successful workshop. The facilitator should avoid killer statements such as, "That is dumb," or, "You what!" and should value or honor statements made by participants. If people open themselves up to share their values and then find that they are "put down," it may be a long time before they are willing to share again.

The setting should be comfortable and roomy. For some groups this may mean chairs, for others, a floor with pillows. Participants should have enough room so that when they break into small groups they are far enough apart not to be disturbed by others. Good ventilation in the room is also essential.

It is important, too, that the facilitator talk about full attention early in the sessions. If a person is talking to the whole group or in a small group, the group members should focus their full attention on that person by maintaining eye contact and allowing the person to speak uninterrupted. Many times, sharing values or experiences from one's life triggers ideas, thoughts, and reactions within others that they want to share immediately by saying things such as, "I know what you mean," or, "Something like that happened to me." However, interrupting cuts off the speaker with the result that she/he feels that her/his particular thought is not valued. By giving full attention to a person, we tell them, "You are worth listening to," and, "I want to hear you."

Formal evaluation for this type of group is difficult because outcomes cannot be measured readily. Value clarification is a process—we hope a life-long process. The style of evaluation used is to ask each participant to write his/her responses to the following stimulus items. This is done at the end of the last meeting.

> I learned . . . .
> I relearned . . . .
> It surprised me to see that I . . . .
> I see that I need to . . . .
> What was the highlight of the session or sessions for
> you? . . . .
> What was the least useful to you? . . . .
> What feedback do you have to give to the facilitator?
> . . . .

Human Sexuality by William Jones

The importance of human sexuality in the scheme of developmental needs requires no documentation. An exemplary structured group aimed at assisting individuals to come to terms with the implications and expression of sexuality in their lives is the following program provided by Bill Jones of the Office of Counseling Services at Gettysburg College, Gettysburg, Pennsylvania.

GROUP FORMAT.   While there are many ways of gathering and disseminating information about sexuality, several factors argue for the use of a small structured group approach. Of primary importance is the belief that sexual facts do not exist without accompanying attitudes or emotions which may alter the ways those facts are perceived. In addition, since human sexuality is such a highly emotional subject, any approach to examining it should deal with the realities of human relationships, life style, self-image, and value structure. A small group approach can offer experiences which foster insight into oneself and the effect one has on others, aid personal unfreezing, provide a more feeling-level orientation, and thus increase the feeling of freedom to share material of a sensitive nature.

In approaching the exercises that follow, the leader should encourage and exemplify critical self-examination and an awareness of fluctuating values. He/she should make it clear that responses from individuals are expected to be varied and that all are acceptable, since "what is" and "what ought to be" are debatable.

The exercises are designed for use in a group of 10 to 12 persons, half of them males and half females. The group meets weekly for an hour and a half for each of eight sessions. A room suitable for maximum interpersonal interaction and large enough for breaking up into smaller subgroups is suggested.

The objectives of this program are as follows:
1. to develop awareness of sexual attitudes and behavior in ourselves and in our culture;
2. to foster freedom to confront honestly, examine, and discuss sexual issues;
3. to provide understanding of factors that inhibit the healthy experiencing of our sexuality;
4. to increase factual information on normal sexual functioning; and
5. to develop positive affirmation of one's sexuality.

SESSION 1.

1. Introduction and community building (30 min.)
    The objectives of this activity are to provide an intro-

duction to the topic and general clarification about expectations, and to provide through use of the "log" an opportunity for the participant to interrelate ideas and experiences which are significant and relevant to the group's objectives. It also gives the leader an opportunity to note the participant's reactions and progress. For both the participant and the leader it can provide indications of growth and change.

a. Explain purposes and format for the sessions that will follow, emphasizing that sexuality encompasses the total personality and is not limited to genitalia. Explain the importance of group members' attendance at all sessions, if possible, because of the shared experiential concept of group process.

b. Present background reading material (Katchadourian & Lunde, 1972).

c. Explain the use of the "log." (The "log" should be a series of entries, to be turned in biweekly, describing the participant's intellectual response to what he/she has seen, read, and heard. Also to be included is what he/she does and feels that is pertinent to the topic of sexuality. There is no required writing style, and entries may vary from one time to the next. They may be subjective, poetic, intellectually critical, or scientific.)

d. Answer questions.

2. Getting acquainted (remainder of session)

The purpose here is to establish group cohesiveness through the sharing of personal data with others, to allow each person to experience taking responsibility for sharing with the group, and to begin the practice of self-disclosure at a relatively safe level. Each participant will need a pencil and paper.

a. Instruct the participants to write a very brief response to the following questions: (1) Besides yourself, who is the most important person in your life right now? (2) Where and from whom did you get your first sex education? (3) Describe a gift someone gave you. (4) What do you hope to gain from being in this group?

b. Instruct the participants to break into subgroups of four or five (depending on the number of participants). Ask each to share his/her name and responses to the four questions with the subgroup members, with each person sharing the response to question number 1 before moving on to subsequent questions.

c. Instruct the subgroups to form one large group. Each individual is to select one other person from his/her subgroup and introduce that individual by telling his/her name and something learned about the person while in the subgroup. Continue this process until all have been introduced.

SESSION 2.

1. Sharing a first sexual experience (45 min.)

The intent of this session is to identify and share common personal feelings and experiences in early childhood, to practice the skill of self-disclosure in a group, and to identify present attitudes about sexual experiences.

Give each participant a straight pin, a pencil and a 3X 5 index card. Instruct the individuals to think about a first "wet dream" or "playing doctor." Ask them to write briefly about the experience on the card and then to pin the card on their chests. Participants should then quietly mill around about the room and read what the others have written, responding nonverbally.

Instruct the participants to gather into groups of five or six and share verbally: (a) what I wrote on my card, (b) how I feel about it now, and (c) how I reacted to what other people wrote.

2. Body image (45 min.)

The aim of the following activity is to encourage the sharing of personal feelings and concerns about the human body, to increase awareness of how society influences attitudes about our bodies, and to encourage giving affirming responses to other persons.

Each group member is given an opportunity to share feelings about his/her body.

a. Going around the circle, one person at a time is asked to stand and share: "how I feel about various parts of my body—hair, chest, face, etc.," both positive and negative feelings. An alternative would be to have participants share a feeling about "the part of my body that I like the least."

b. If the feelings are negative, the leader asks where the negative feelings come from ("Who says so?" "Where did you learn that small breasts were bad?" etc.).

c. The group is instructed to give positive (truthful) feedback to each individual (e.g., "I never really noticed your hips," "You have such a warm face," etc.).

SESSION 3. The "dirty words" game (90 min.)

The idea behind this exercise is to lower group inhibitions and heighten group openness in sharing words (to desensitize). Also, this activity can serve to make it easier to talk about sex in a mixed group by legitimizing various language forms, and to build group spirit through use of a team game. Finally, it can enable group members to talk about their feelings in explicit terms.

1. Introduction: Sexuality as a subject has spawned many language forms. Often in our culture we find it embarrassing or uncomfortable to use various kinds of words to describe parts of the body or various kinds of sexual activity. For example, we often describe our sexual appendages as "things" or "it." As children we may have called our penis or vagina by a variety of "family" terms. We are not always familiar or comfortable with scientific terms like "coitus," for example. Often our language is vague with

imprecise terms like "doing it" or "making out." In addition, our culture is filled with vernacular or so-called "dirty words" such as fuck, cock, pussy, etc., which are often (but not always) used demeaningly.

2. Form two groups of five or six persons. You may wish to give them team names.

3. Each group is told that the members are to respond to several sexual terms by coming up with as many synonyms for that word as possible. One person in each group is to be selected as recorder to write down the words as they are spoken. Any term that is synonomous with the key word is appropriate. The team with the most words when time is called is the "winner." First word is "intercourse."

(An alternative: Place a large piece of blank paper on the wall and as each individual comes up with a synonym, he/she stands up, states the word loudly enough for everyone to hear, and writes it on the paper with a magic marker. The result is often a hilarious race to list the most terms.)

4. After several minutes, the leader calls time and asks each recorder to count the team's words. The team with the most words reads off its list of synonyms for "intercourse." The losing group is asked to share the words on its list not mentioned by the winning group.

5. Give the next word, "penis," and repeat Step 4. Other key words may be "vagina," "homosexual," or "masturbation."

6. Ask the entire group to process the exercise by asking: What were your feelings during this exercise? Was it difficult to say certain words? How did you feel about the presence of the opposite sex? Did you notice any particular patterns in the way you felt about some words?

7. The leader may wish to point out some factors that make a "dirty word" dirty, building on the notion that these are limiting, often self-deceiving forms of expression that reveal insecurity rather than mere unconventionality. Reasons behind the employment of these so-called "dirty

words" include the attempt to gain a psychological advantage over another by shocking, insulting, frightening, fascinating, or in some way "overpowering" the listener emotionally. Also, conforming to convention, seeking emotional release and reassurance, and not knowing other, more proper or anatomically descriptive terms motivate some people to use "dirty words" extensively.

SESSION 4. Sharing of childhood memories (90 min.)

The objectives of this session are to identify and express to others some personal experiences and feelings related to sexuality, to increase awareness of how personal attitudes about sexuality develop, to discover the universality of most sexual feelings and experiences, to practice the skill of self-disclosure within a small group, and to identify how one's present attitudes and feelings toward sex are related to earlier experience. This exercise is also described in Morrison and Price (1974).

1. Have available newsprint on which to write cues for discussion. Instruct participants to form mixed sex trios, and if possible not to group with close friends or partners from earlier discussion groups. Have each trio find a private space and give them the option of not sharing, but suggest that they may want to make a mental note of the feelings that may come to mind so that they can be dealt with later, privately.

2. The following comments will serve to introduce the exercise: "In learning about human sexuality, the biological aspects of sex and reproduction are certainly important. But equally significant are the affective aspects—the attitudes, feelings, taboos which we privately have about sexuality. These are learned mostly from our families and also from the street—from our peers as we are growing up. Today we are going to share some of these experiences and memories. You may have difficulty recalling experiences in

a particular area; you may have blocked out experiences and feelings, perhaps because you learned they were bad or dirty. You may also find that someone else's sharing triggers a flood of memories you had forgotten about. You may also discover that there are some experiences which you prefer not to share with your group. Share only what you wish to share. You may want to let your partners know you are reticent about speaking, even though you have decided to share. You may want to note those actions or statements which make you feel ill at ease in your group."

3.   In this section, it is wise to move quickly through the first three questions and increase the time allotment as the exercise develops. Before sharing, advise the participants first to take a few minutes for reflection.

a.   "What feelings do you recall about being a girl or being a boy and how did you feel toward children of the opposite sex (envy, disdain)? Did your parents expect different things of you than they expected of your sisters (brothers)? If so, how did you feel about that?" (5-min. pause)

b.   "What were your family patterns in regard to talk about sex, nudity, physical expression of affection?" (7-min. pause)

c.   "What memories do you have of sex play as a child? If your parents were aware of it, what did they say or do? What were your feelings about sex play?" (Continue to increase time on these subjects, allowing a few minutes for reflection before each one.)

d.   "When did you first become aware of your parents' sexuality? How? What feelings did you have?"

e.   "What memories do you have of approaching adolescence, menstruation, wet dreams, awareness of sexual feelings, body development (or lack of it)? What were your feelings at the time?"

f.   "What are your memories of the first time you were kissed or touched by a member of the opposite sex? What do you recall about your first love? Your first serious sexual involvement?"

g.   "What was your most pleasurable or memorable sexual experience? This experience may be alone, relating to your sense of yourself as a man or woman; or it may be with another (not necessarily a genital experience)."

h.   "In what ways is your 'personal history' related to your present feelings about your own sexuality?"

SESSION 5. True-false sexuality quiz (90 min.)

The purpose here is to increase factual information about normal sexual functioning and dispel many of the myths surrounding human sexuality, to help group members be aware of their own level of sexual knowledge, and to share more completely factual sexual information.

1.   Hand out true-false sexuality quiz. Ask students to form dyads and decide, as teams, which answers are true or false.

2.   Ask the group to form a circle with "teams" sitting together.

3.   Go through the list of statements by going around the circle and having each team state their response. Ask for general group agreement or disagreement on response. If the response is incorrect, the leader shares the correct response. Many statements will initiate more elaborate discussion, and this should be encouraged. The following are ten examples from a set of 60 true-false items constructed for this exercise. A good source of material for such items and answers to them is McCary (1971).

a.   Women ejaculate as men do.
b.   Simultaneous orgasms are more satisfactory than those experienced separately and are, moreover, necessary for sexual compatibility in marriage.

   c.   Women are capable of multiple orgasms.

   d.   It is dangerous to have sexual intercourse during menstruation.

   e.   Sexual dysfunction is much more frequently a matter of psychological factors than of physiological disturbance.

   f.   Alcohol is a sexual stimulant.

   g.   Sex desire and ability decrease markedly after the age of 40 to 50.

   h.   There is no absolutely "safe" period for sexual intercourse insofar as conception is concerned.

   i.   The birth-control pill will eventually cause a wide variety of ills in any woman using it for any length of time.

   j.   Masturbation is known to cause many physical and psychological problems.

SESSION 6. Sex roles: The ideal man—the ideal woman (90 min.)

This activity is designed to assist participants to learn what roles members of the opposite sex ascribe to one another, to dispel some of the culturally preconceived notions about how males and females feel about one another, to assist participants to share personal feelings about one's sex role in a mixed group, and to help them be more empathic and make fewer generalizations about the opposite sex.

1.   Divide participants into all male and all female groups, assign each group a meeting place, and give them magic markers and poster paper.

   a.   Each group brainstorms and writes down the qualities of the ideal man (for women) or the ideal woman (for men) (15 min.).

b.   Each group is asked to imagine what the group of the opposite sex might list. Women are asked to list what men think is the ideal woman; men are asked to list what women think is the ideal man (15 min).

c.   Each group is asked to list the desired attributes of their own sex, i.e., men, the ideal man; women, the ideal female (15 min.).

2.   Everyone reconvenes. Each group's lists are posted on the wall, and a spokesperson explains the terms. The groups begin with number 1 until all groups have reported. Then they move to number 2, etc. (45 min.).

3.   Some variation on the above may be desirable. In option 1, participants break up into two groups (mixed gender). One group sits in a small circle and the other in a larger circle around the smaller group. The inside group has a general reaction session sharing feelings, attitudes, beliefs, etc., for about 20 minutes. The outside group observes and remains silent. After time is up, the groups switch positions. After another 20 minutes, both groups discuss the entire exercise.

In option 2, women and men break into separate groups and role play a dorm or floor meeting where they assume the roles of the opposite sex. The men (playing women) may wish to discuss the social situation from a woman's point of view and vice versa.

SESSION 7. Reactions to films (90 min.).

The objectives of this session are to increase individual awareness of sexual attitudes, to share individual interpretations of abstract concepts and explore feeling content of these interpretations, to express feelings about symbolic representations of sexual themes, and to discover the varieties of attitudes toward sexual themes in a given group.

1.   Divide the group into two subgroups before the films. (Suggested films: "Orange," "A Quickie," "Unfolding," all available from Multi Media Resource Center, 540 Powell Street, San Francisco, California 94018.)

2.   Immediately after viewing the films, hand each individual paper and writing materials. Instruct the participants to complete the following sentence for each film: "This film made me feel that sex is like . . ." Participants should use their imaginations freely as they consider the feelings generated by the films. An example of such a response might be: "This film made me feel that sex is like a roller coaster ride—fast and furious."

3.   When all participants have completed their sentences for each film, ask each one to fold his/her paper and put it in the center of the circle. Then each is asked to draw out as many pieces of paper as there were films.

4.   Each person reads the first sentence he/she has drawn from the common pile, and attempts to share what he/she thinks the writer was trying to express. The writer then identifies her/himself and shares what she/he was really trying to express and what aspects of the film stimulated those comments.

5.   Follow the same procedure for all of the sentence completions.

SESSION 8. Sharing of final log entry (90 min.).

The purposes of this session include giving the participants an opportunity to share their growth and learnings with other group members, enabling each group member to give feedback to the leader about his or her experience, enabling group members to express how in-group learnings have affected their outside experiences, and discovering to what extent the goals of the program have been met.

Participants are asked to bring their final "log" entry (see Session 1) and share its contents with the entire group.

This "log" entry should provide an overview and final reaction to the series of group sessions.

Loneliness and Self-Betrayal by Victor Atyas

One typical intrapersonal theme which has become the focus of structured developmental group efforts is loneliness. The next few pages describe a workshop entitled "Loneliness and Self-Betrayal." This program is the creation of Victor Atyas in the Office of Counseling and Student Development at the University of Rhode Island, Kingston. Following are the elements of this program as described by Atyas.

GROUP FORMAT.   For most people, and particularly for students at the college level, loneliness is an issue of great importance. This is not loneliness caused by geographical isolation, but loneliness brought about by self-abuse, a sexist orientation to life, social role playing, or other abortive ways of finding meaning for oneself. Because feeling lonely is both painful and often humiliating, those so afflicted are under great pressure to seek escape, an escape they usually find by becoming more vigorously engaged in behavior which leads to self-fragmentation. Loneliness leads to self-betrayal, and self-betrayal to even greater loneliness. Indiscriminate relationships can only increase one's state of alienation and feeling of ultimate futility.

Participation in a workshop on loneliness and self-betrayal should give individuals an opportunity to become exposed to honest and genuine interpersonal relating, to become aware of their tendency to compromise their integrity, and to discover more authentic ways of being themselves.

The design proposed here is flexible. It can be applied to groups consisting of as few as four participants, or up to ten times that many. Of course, the larger the number, the bigger the physical facilities required. The time allocated for the total workshop can involve half a day, a full day, or two days, depending on the needs of the participants. My own preference is for four hours. There are no particular criteria for selecting potential members. As this workshop is typically offered to a college population, the assumption may be made that intellectual levels and age will not vary widely. It is preferable to have approximately equal numbers of men and women so that as eventual subgroups are formed there will be an opportunity to deal with self-betrayal which results from the consequences of narrowly conceptualized roles of being a male or a female. The only individuals not suited to involvement in such an experience are those who are clearly emotionally handicapped, and who are in need of active psychological or psychiatric care.

The workshop should begin only when all participants have arrived and the doors can be closed. A most essential factor for its success is the mood created by the leader. She/he will want to convey the seriousness of the enterprise, without being stuffy or overly intellectual about it. Typically, the leader will call for silence and try to make eye contact with most of the participants before addressing herself/himself to the tasks ahead. She/he should welcome them, introduce her/himself to them, and then ask them to look around for a place to which they feel they can retreat that will give them the feeling that they "belong" there. They then move to the chosen place, where they are invited to make themselves comfortable, but not to engage anyone in conversation. Such a procedure usually leads to a mood for introspection and reflection.

When the participants have found places in the room where they are relatively undistracted and can become absorbed in themselves, the leader should give four 5X7 index cards and a pencil to each person. She/he then asks that the participants give their attention to their immediate emotional state, reflecting on how they feel about being in that place, and on their expectations. They have five minutes to get in touch with themselves, at the end of which they note their introspective feelings on Card No. 1.

After two minutes or so, it is a good idea for the leader to stress the fact that in a workshop like this one it is especially important to be honest about oneself. Participants might be gently encouraged to self-disclose by being reminded that they will get as much out of the experience as they put into it.

Following this, the leader invites them to go back into themselves, and to reflect for another five minutes on what loneliness means to them. She/he tells them not to intellectualize, but to seek "in their guts" for a personally meaningful definition. Because most people are not accustomed to such introspection, it might be helpful to say (after a few minutes have passed), "If thinking of what loneliness means to you is difficult, concentrate on a specific time in your life when you felt painfully lonely and try to recall how your mind and body felt." If even this approach to getting in touch with their loneliness is not sufficient for the participants, the leader might suggest that they think of themselves as movie directors attempting to portray a scene depicting a lonely man or woman. At the end of five minutes, the leader should ask them to describe on Card No. 2 whatever discovery they have made within themselves as to what loneliness is like for them, or to depict graphically what a lonely state is like.

After they have finished this task, the leader instructs them to go back into themselves still a third time, and to think for five minutes or so of an actual time when they felt oppressed by loneliness, and this time to focus on what they did to cope with this feeling. A few minutes later, she/he may invite them to reflect on whether they have any typical, consistent ways of acting to reduce loneliness. At the end of five minutes, participants are asked to write on Card No. 3 what they usually tend to do when feeling lonely.

After they have finished writing their thoughts, the leader asks them to go back into themselves a fourth time, and to think of an instance when they felt very lonely but were able to engage in a behavior which eventually resulted in a feeling of some fullness and well-being for themselves, a strategy which seemed to work to help abate the loneliness. After about two minutes, the leader might want to emphasize the fact that this time they are being asked to think of a way they coped with loneliness which led to a feeling of pride or positive regard for themselves. When the allotted time has passed, she/he asks them to describe on Card No. 4 the result of this introspection. This concludes the introductory phase of the workshop.

The next phase is directed at processing the material with other people. The leader invites the participants to look around the room, and to begin the process of getting acquainted. She/he encourages them to walk around and make contact, but not to discuss what they have written on their cards. Naturally, the length of this exercise will depend on the duration of the workshop. Usually, five to ten minutes are enough for the participants to get a feeling for the people with whom they would like to interact. They should be encouraged to move along and not to spend all their time with any one person. When it seems that they have loosened up, a suggestion should be made that they now select one particular person with whom they would like to spend some time. After pairs are formed, the leader asks that three pairs merge with each other so that there will be subgroups of six people each. There is room for some flexibility here. Some leaders may prefer to have smaller, more intimate groups consisting of as few as four members, and other leaders may prefer groups of eight or even more. The less total time the participants will have to spend together, the more beneficial the smaller size groups will be.

After the subgroups are formed, the leader instructs

them to find relatively secluded spots, or separate rooms if available, so that they will not disturb each other. Then the members of each subgroup are invited to take turns reading Card No. 1, then, when finished, Card No. 2, then Card No. 3, and finally Card No. 4. It is important that the leader remind the participants to respond actively and openly to each other as they take turns sharing the material on the cards. She/he should emphasize that the more candid the feedback process is, the more meaningful the involvement will be, and the greater the opportunities for personal growth.

The leader's function, for the remainder of the workshop, will be to visit the individual subgroups and to become a resource person to them. After the subgroups have begun to interact, the leader does just that—goes from group to group and facilitates the group process. She/he stays as long as her/his services seem to be needed, attempting always to facilitate the interaction with her/his presence, and not to hamper it. Some groups very quickly develop a momentum of their own, and no contribution is needed from the leader. On the other hand, there are instances where one must participate actively before group members can get on with their work. Depending on the needs, the group leader may ask provocative questions, share her/his own experiences, comment on the prevailing moods of the group, or empathically relate to individual members.

This phase of the workshop can last anywhere from three hours to one and-a-half days, or even more. There is actually no limit to how long the group interaction can proceed, for, after all the cards have been read, the opportunity for a spontaneous interaction among members of a group is somewhat limitless. New issues may be raised and discussed at will. It is important, though, that in all groups time be allowed for the processing of their experience. At the end of this phase of the workshop, the leader invites all the participants to join her/him in a total group discussion. In the large group, it is desirable to continue the processing of interactions, because (inevitably) there will be individuals who will not have been able to reach a sense of closure during their participation in the small groups. They should be encouraged to articulate their feelings and reactions at this time so as to complete the integration of their experience. The large group experience will also help the leader to gauge the success of the workshop, and to make possible plans for a follow-up.

Loneliness is the fate of human beings who have lost their autonomy, and who cannot differentiate between behavior which is conducive to personal growth and behavior which leads to self-degradation. Escape is the dominant mode of adjustment. In the course of the workshop, it is hoped that the members will have taken advantage of the opportunity to transcend their loneliness, at least temporarily, through meaningful involvement. They should have attained greater self-awareness as to the causes and consequences of loneliness, and have become more aware of the vicious cycle between loneliness and self-betrayal. Finally, if they have gone deeply enough into themselves, they should have experienced the awakening of a new value system, one which places greater worth on solitude with integrity than on avoidance of loneliness through self-betrayal.

The key variable to the success of this kind of workshop seems to be the type of mood which permeates it, and the leader has the major responsibility for establishing this mood. It appears to be essential for the success of the workshop that the leader be able to create an atmosphere conducive to introspection, personal honesty, and willingness to risk self-exposure. She/he has to be involved in the interactions, and has to convey an uncompromising sense of integrity. Should she/he in any way convey an attitude of indifference, or a need for self-aggrandizement, of having to be in control, or of desiring to be entertained, the experience will end in failure. Benefits can be derived both from a short-term workshop and from one of longer duration. The major value of a half-day workshop is the opportunity it provides for learning experientially that loneliness is something shared by many, and that it can be transcended by relating honestly with people who are, themselves, willing to be honest. The full day or longer workshop, while making it possible to have a more fulfilling interpersonal encounter, also presents a unique opportunity for a deeper examination of the vulnerability which often leads to self-betrayal, and of ways of coping with loneliness which assure one's self-respect and personal wholeness.

Raising the Male Consciousness by Richard C. Nelson and Allen E. Segrist

A theme group designed to assist men to explore their maleness is the following program. The male CR (Consciousness Raising) group is the work of Richard C. Nelson and Allen E. Segrist, both of the Counseling and Personnel Services Department at Purdue University, West Lafayette, Indiana.

GROUP FORMAT.   This program is intended for males who are interested in gaining greater understanding of themselves, the effects of being born male, and ways of relating comfortably and openly with others in light of their maleness. Membership is restricted to men only, with one facilitator for every eight participants. An ideal setting for the sessions is a carpeted, informal area with flexible seating arrangements, large enough to accommodate the total number enrolled. The group can be organized for an extended session of 12 hours, for a full weekend, or in weekly three-hour sessions spread over several months.

The units for this structured group format are "stages" which may be explored, as noted earlier, in one intensive workshop or in several meetings over an extended time period. While a series of miscellaneous activities will not necessarily produce an effective male consciousness group, on the other hand, an effective group can utilize activities which then produce personally relevant dialog. The group benefits from the processing which follows the active experiencing of self and others. The stages which provide for this active experiencing comprise a developmental learning sequence which is generally applicable to all participants; specific activities can be modified and applied to meet the needs of the particular group.

An overall goal is stated at the outset. It encompasses the global objective of enabling participants to develop their feelings of comfort and their effectiveness in dealing with their own world and that of others. Awareness and acceptance of a number of components are needed by each member for resolution of this theme. These include:

1. the concept of humanness and of being a person in our society;
2. the responsibilities, advantages, and difficulties of being male in our society;
3. sexuality trends and changes within society; and
4. implications and integration of these components for the person.

The activities described below are to be used selectively and to the extent needed to stimulate interaction and exploration of relevant issues; in no way should they be viewed as substitutes for dialogue. We encourage the development of an active, caring, and gentle atmosphere to promote discussion of the kinds of changes males need to implement in their lives today. Such group experiences with other males are likely to encourage a deeper understanding and a richer acceptance of self and others.

STAGE 1. Exploration of growing up a male

Objective: To understand how we have
                          learned about and accepted or re-
                          jected masculine role expecta-
                          tions.

Possible Activities:

1. *Brainstorming.* Members brainstorm from a prea-dolescent perspective: "Boys are . . ." "Girls are . . ." and from a present perspective: "Men should (Women shouldn't) . . ." "Men shouldn't (Women should) . . ."

2. *Fantasy.* Members fantasize five-year-olds playing at the beach, in sandbox, etc., illustrating how male roles are learned.

3. *Written recall of personal experiences.* Members write about sexual information input as a child; learning about physical development; learning about masculine behaviors.

4. *Role play.* Members illustrate what males are sup-posed to do in specific situations in their roles as son, father, husband, employer, etc.; in an argument, at a fu-neral, at a ball game, etc.

5. *Listening.* Members write a list of topics which are "OK" and "not OK" to discuss with others.

6. *Innocuous topics.* To prove that it is possible, and to encourage males to be verbally expressive, dyads discuss innocuous topics assigned at random in two-minute dia-logues. Sample topics: post, ear, lead, etc.

7. *Role Reversal.* In a reversal of sex role, one member of a dyad assumes the place of a woman: dating, at home, as a mother, etc.; then roles are exchanged.

Materials: Paper, pencil
Assignments: Diary or journal involving obser-
                          vation, further recall, personal
                          feelings.

STAGE 2. Intimacy with self and others

Objective: To help us experience both the freedom and the reasonable limits of intimacy.

Possible Activities:

1. *Quaker meeting.* Eyes are closed. Each person is invited to answer these questions: Whom do you see as important in your past? How do they want you to be or think you should be? How do you feel? What do you want to do? How do you want to be? Answer these questions for the present.

2. *Circle of awareness.* Small groups express their feelings nonverbally through their hands. See Stevens (1971, p. 214 ff).

3. *Dyadic interview.* Group members interview each other. See Pfeiffer and Jones (1969, pp. 97–107).

4. *Triad.* Groups of three discuss five statements of "qualities I like about myself," and three statements of "ways I withhold from others."

Materials: None

Assignments: Continue diary or journal emphasizing personal experiences with intimacy, reflecting upon feelings within and outside of the group.

STAGE 3. Choice awareness

Objective: To understand that our caring and ruling behaviors are choices we have made that we can change.

Possible Activities:

1. *Ruling choice dyad.* How you use rank, power, age,

seniority; how you respond to the ruling choices of others; how you own, control, or manage others.

2.   *Yes–No dyads.* Palms together, one says "yes," the other "no," several times; then reverse statements.

3.   *Mirroring with hands.* One person ruling, the other ruled; reverse.

4.   *Pair role play.* One stands over the other; reverse; then stand as equals.

5.   *Caring choice dyad.* Assign to the other person the role of someone important to you. What caring do you want to give, receive, avoid, withhold? Express verbally or nonverbally the caring you feel for that person.

6.   *Pair caring.* One gives the other the caring he wants the other to have; reverse.

Materials:	See Nelson and Bloom (1975) for further activities.
Assignments:	Observation of personal choices, the implementation of different choices, examining personal feelings, updating the diary or journal.

STAGE 4. Relationships

Objective:	To help us interact with others in caring ways and to speak to the relationship.
Possible Activities:	

1.   *Statements to group members.* Relationship statements are shared by each person within the group: "This group is . . ." "My feeling right now is . . ." "My feelings toward you now are . . ."

2.   *Sociogram in a fishbowl.* In turn, each person stands in the center of the group with eyes closed while others

position themselves to express their relationship to him.

    3.   *Reverse sociogram.* Focus person arranges others where and how he sees them in relation to himself.

    4.   *Dyad.* Each member of the pair completes the statement: "What I want from you right now is . . ."

Materials:	None
Assignments:	Continue journal or diary by exploring and considering personal relationships and feelings for others.

STAGE 5. Training for touching

Objective:	To help us to express our difficulties with, and experience our need for, touching.

Possible Activities:

    1.   *Role play.* Recall where touching messages came from, and role-play experiences between son and dad, son and mother, male and male friends, male and female friends. Illustrate both "OK" and "not OK" touching messages.

    2.   *Blind milling.* Mill around blindly and nonverbally in darkened room. Move first without, and then with, touching.

    3.   *Active–passive lineup.* Form facing lines and rotate after every 1 or 2 minutes. Persons in the active line act out touching contact while passive persons receive, until all group members experience both active and passive modes with all other members. Communicate feelings of the relationship through touching.

Materials:	None
Assignments:	Continue journal or diary by exploring the "touch" and "don't

touch" messages within the group and beyond it; consider related feelings.

STAGE 6. Functioning in the here and now

Objective:

To help us give and receive direct, current messages and to help with leave taking.

Possible Activities:

1. *Role play and reality.* Members act out negatives, such as rejection, denial, uncaring, dominating, etc.; then switch to open and honest statements that are person relevant.

2. *Group impressions.* With eyes closed, members sit in a circle and are asked to point to another, "of whom I'm most afraid," "to whom I feel most attracted as a human being," "who seems strongest," "who seems softest," etc. On signal eyes are opened and discussion follows.

3. *Written feedback.* Each person writes a signed note to each other person in the group, striving for relevant positive and negative feedback.

4. *Specifying a contract.* Each group member specifies a personal contract he will accomplish: "I will make more caring, fewer ruling choices," "I will stop trying to prove myself so much," etc.

5. *Saying goodbye.* Each member says what is up-to-date for the relationships involved, leaving nothing important unsaid. All affirm their being OK beyond the limits of the group. Each person takes his leave.

Materials: Paper, pencil.
Assignments: Develop further awareness goals

and acceptance of self in everyday life.

At the end of the group's final session, personal statements, journals, and written feedback comments are shared to assess the significance and success of the program, and to aid in the planning of future groups.

Self-Esteem Workshop by Stanley Hunt and Stanley Pavey

Another group in this category is designed for persons experiencing difficulties because of an inadequate sense of self-esteem. The workshop described here was developed by Stanley Hunt and Stanley Pavey at the Counseling Center of the University of Maryland, College Park, and the following is their elaboration of the workshop design.

GROUP FORMAT.   The Self-Esteem Workshop is designed for clients who consciously devalue themselves. Harsh self-criticism for failures to meet their own standards characterizes these persons, accompanied frequently by feelings of inferiority, inadequacy, and guilt or shame. The workshop is not meant for clients experiencing chronic depression or severe obsessional problems, nor for those who suffer from psychotic or borderline conditions. People who are engaged in ongoing individual counseling are usually excellent candidates and will benefit from the efforts required in the workshop. While both male and female participation is desirable, it does not seem to be essential.

The workshop is planned for six or eight clients who meet weekly with two coleaders. Each of the first seven sessions requires at least one-and-a-half hours, although a two-hour meeting time is preferable. An eighth follow-up meeting occurs from four to six weeks after the seventh meeting for purposes of encouraging sustained self-enhancement behaviors and for evaluation. Obtaining client commitment to attendance at the seven working sessions is essential.

The workshop is primarily behavioral in conception and organization, although techniques are influenced by Gestalt and ego-analytic thinking as well. The aim is to teach participants to use a variety of techniques to disrupt habituated patterns of self-devaluation and to develop self-enhancing alternatives. Even though referral criteria bring members to the group who are aware of their self-criticism, it is necessary to sensitize them to the harshness and extent of their self-devaluing thoughts and emotions. As clients increase their awareness of the habits of self-criticism, they are better prepared to attempt to break these habits. Group discussion serves to broaden the individual's judgmental perspectives and to encourage efforts at self-change by offering peer and leader approval. Through structured exercises in the group, clients learn techniques for breaking self-devaluing habits. Homework between sessions encourages the practice of techniques introduced in the group. This practice is reviewed at the beginning of each subsequent session in order to encourage evaluation of effects and refinement of application. No specific time frames are offered for each of the exercises described, but leaders can experiment with roughly equal time allotments for each segment within the total time given.

SESSION 1

1. Introduction and obtaining commitment.

The leaders introduce themselves, the goals for the workshop, and the nature of the structured experiences. They encourage each member to introduce her/himself and to assess the appropriateness of the workshop for her/-his problems. Those who do not find the workshop appropriate or who cannot commit themselves to the seven sessions may leave the group at this point.

2. Pride-shame lists and discussion of the basis for self-judgment.

Each participant is asked to list on paper five attributes "that make you most proud about yourself" and five "that make you most ashamed of yourself." It may be necessary for the leaders to encourage completion of the "proud" list. The lists are collected by the leaders who use the items, without identifying the authors of the lists, to stimulate group discussion of what makes people worthwhile. The leaders attempt to obtain participation by all members in this discussion. It is typically necessary for the leaders to challenge the assumption that human worth is determined solely by achievements.

3. Relaxation training.

Training in complete muscular relaxation is introduced by the leaders. We employ the cassette tape by Arnold Lazarus (Instructional Dynamics Institute Basic Relaxation Exercises) with the clients lying down. The leaders explain that relaxation is a pleasurable experience within a client's control, and suggest that individuals may thus learn to feel better about themselves without needing an instrumental goal. Following training, members are encouraged to begin daily practice of their relaxation exercises.

4. Homework: Keeping a record of "put-downs."

The leaders distribute daily record forms to the clients and offer instruction in the recording of self-devaluing thoughts and statements (put-downs). They define and discuss methods of regular recording between sessions. The leaders express the hope that clients will sensitize themselves to their self-devaluation through self-observation and that they attempt to discover events which stimulate undue self-criticism. It is made clear that the homework will be collected and discussed at the next session (simple forms can be made up and copied).

SESSION 2

1. Review of Homework

The leaders collect the daily records of put-downs and quickly review them. They encourage the group to discuss the difficulties and discoveries of self-criticism. It is wise to try to elicit responses from all members, to model approval of record keeping and self-awareness, and to confront directly any resistance to the assigned task.

2. Alternatives to put-downs: "I'm OK"

Because clients are more apt to justify their self-criticism than to imagine self-enhancing alternatives, it is appropriate to begin with a simple technique which permits a self-enhancing statement or thought to replace a self-critical thought. The leaders teach clients to add the thought, "... but I'm OK" to every put-down. For example, "I'm not as smart as he is, but I'm OK. ..." or, "I didn't study as much as I could have for the exam, but I'm OK. ..." Each member should attempt to practice replacing a self-criticism with the " ... but I'm OK" statement in the session.

3. Relaxation and fantasy of "I'm OK ..."

Clients are again asked to relax physically while recumbent. A brief review of the muscle groups is helpful to clients at this stage, and serves to reinforce their week's practice in relaxation. After they are relaxed, clients are instructed to imagine a situation in which they put themselves down and to practice adding the self-enhancing thought, " ... but I'm OK." Repetitions of this task serve to associate the pleasurable feelings of relaxation with an attitude of self-acceptance.

4. Homework: Paying self a compliment.

The new homework assignment for this session requires that clients pay themselves a compliment at least once daily in the course of normal conversation. Typically, clients find this a frightening assignment and need practice in the session as well as ample encouragement from the leaders. Brief pairing of clients in practicing compliments is advisable in order to avoid the anxiety of complimenting oneself in the total group.

Daily record sheets are again distributed to assist the clients in recording their put-downs and self-accepting replacement statements during the week. A section of the daily records should be set aside for recording their daily self-compliments.

SESSION 3

1.   Review of homework.

The leaders again collect and review clients' daily record sheets. Discussion of the homework may best be begun by questioning group members about their reactions to the assignment. The leaders thus begin to recognize individual success and to confront individual resistance to the tasks. For some members, paying oneself a compliment is equivalent to boasting or bragging. The leaders may be helpful by suggesting that there is nothing wrong with self-compliments.

2.   Correcting projections: "I see–I imagine" technique.

Some participants have developed the habit of projecting harsh self-judgment onto others. The "I see–I imagine" technique, borrowed from Gestalt therapy, is introduced to assist these clients in differentiating sensory data from personal interpretation. The leaders model the technique by one leader paying her/himself a compliment and reporting on what is perceived and what is interpreted from the other leader's response. The leader who is reporting is also offering a model for comparing his/her personal interpretation with the actual thoughts and feelings of the other person, i.e. "checking out" the other's reaction instead of assuming that it is negative.

Following instruction, group members pair up to practice the "I see–I imagine" technique by having one partner pay her/himself a compliment, then report both what she/he observed and what she/he imagined in the partner's response. Partners are expected to describe their actual thoughts and feelings to help each other to check out interpretations. Pairs should reverse roles after each turn, and each member should practice at least three compliments and "I see–I imagine" analyses.

Group discussion of reactions to this technique should follow the practice in pairs. This may be a difficult exercise for clients who do not project their self-criticism onto others.

3.   Homework: Practice in checking out others' reactions.

The new assignment for the week requires clients to record their perceptions and interpretations of their friends' reactions after they have paid themselves a compliment, following the "I see–I imagine" principles. At least one compliment and analysis per day is expected. The leaders urge clients to check out their interpretations with their friends when they feel able, as they have practiced in the session.

Daily record sheets are distributed so that clients can continue to record their put-downs and self-enhancing "I'm OK" statements or thoughts. The section of the record where daily self-compliments are recorded should remind clients to perform the "I see–I imagine" analysis of friends' reactions.

SESSION 4

1.   Review of Homework.

Although daily record sheets are collected, the leaders concentrate more upon eliciting individual reports of progress to the group. Group members should become more proficient at praising each other for success. Since the "I see–I imagine" technique is difficult for some members, the leaders should understand this difficulty and look for other aspects of the homework to examine and praise.

2. Further practice of the "I see–I imagine" technique.

Members pair up with different partners from last session to obtain further practice in self-compliment and analysis of their partner's reactions. Even for clients who do not project self-criticism, this practice serves to enhance the attitude that self-compliments are appropriate and acceptable to others.

3. Relaxation associated with pleasurable fantasy.

Most clients will now be reasonably adept at achieving muscular relaxation in the session. The leaders instruct the group first to imagine putting themselves down, then to interrupt the put-down with a fantasy of themselves in a pleasurable situation of their own choosing. At first, the pleasurable scene may reflect instrumental achievement, so the leaders may encourage attempts at imagining pleasurable scenes which do not involve instrumental behaviors. This technique goes beyond the " . . . but I'm OK" technique in helping the client to interrupt put-downs with a self-enhancing response involving both pleasurable feelings and an attitude of self-approval.

4. Homework: Practice with pleasurable fantasy.

Daily record sheets distributed to clients are modified to encourage the interruption of put-downs with a pleasurable fantasy rather than with the " . . . but I'm OK" thoughts of previous assignments. The leaders stress that, while both techniques for interrupting self-criticism are acceptable, this week's practice should emphasize the use of self-enhancing fantasy. In addition, recording of self-compliments is expected to increase, so more space is allowed for recording of incidents involving self-compliments in communication with others.

SESSION 5

1.   Review of homework.

It is important for the leaders to continue to collect and review the daily record sheets. Resistance to homework practice tends to become more obvious by this time and should be confronted directly. It is expected that clients will have had differing success in interrupting put-downs with pleasurable fantasy. Group members can be helpful in approving of their fellow members' attempts, regardless of successful accomplishment.

2.   Defense against criticism by others.

Although these clients are typically their own worst critics, most have been exposed to others who find fault with them. The leaders describe the use of a self-enhancing statement as a defense against criticism by others. The leaders should model self-enhancing responses with each other. The group members are then paired with new partners to practice mild criticism and self-enhancing responses. They then reconvene for general discussion of the experience. There may be some hurt feelings to be assuaged and understood in the group.

3.   Covert rehearsal of defense against criticism.

Clients are requested to relax deeply while recumbent, and to imagine a situation in which they are criticized by another person. In fantasy, they are to practice responding with a self-enhancing statement, as they have done in reality with their partners. The leaders thus introduce the technique of covert rehearsal to help clients anticipate situations in which they expect to feel disapproval. Since the clients may arrange their contemporary lives to avoid critical friends, the leaders may have to suggest situations in which authorities (such as parents or teachers) are apt to be critical.

4.   Homework: Practice in covert rehearsal.

The new element of the homework requires daily practice of relaxed fantasy in which the client imagines criticism from others and imagines a self-enhancing response. The daily record sheets also call for continued practice in interruption of put-downs with pleasurable fantasy or " . . . but I'm OK." Practice in self-compliments is also to be continued and recorded.

SESSION 6

1. Review of the homework.

Given the difficulties that some clients experience with covert rehearsal practice, it is wise to begin this session's review with reports of practice in compliments and interruptions of put-downs. It is then easier for the group to respond differentially to their experience with attempts at covert rehearsal. Discussion of covert rehearsal may bring out some clients' habit of feeling disapproved of when they decline another's request for new responsibilities. This discussion can pave the way for the next activity in the workshop.

2. "I should—I want" exercise.

The leaders briefly introduce distinctions between obligations and personal desires. Then clients are paired with different partners. The task is to list aloud to the partner those things that one feels she/he should do or like, then those that one wants to do or like. The partner then has the task of noting similarities and differences among items on the two lists.

As the group reconvenes for discussion, it usually becomes apparent that many clients find their lists of obligations to be extensive and their wants to have become confused with obligations. The leaders then try to help members begin to make more clear distinctions between "shoulds" and "wants." They also are helping clients to observe and question their attitudes about responsibility and conscientiousness.

3. Homework: Replacing "should" with "want."

This session's assignment requests clients to make a daily record of things they feel they ought to be doing and a list of things they feel they would really like to do. A separate list is made of things clients are doing that they do not want to do. At least once or twice a day, the client tries to substitute doing something she/he would like to do for something she/he feels obligated to do.

The daily record sheets also encourage continued practice in interruption of put-downs and in application of self-enhancing behavior (self-compliments and covert or active self-enhancement in response to others' criticism).

SESSION 7

1. Review of homework.

Since this is the final working session, the leaders are shifting responsibility for maintaining practice in self-enhancement from themselves and the group to the individual member. The initial topic is the "I should–I want" recording and substitution practiced during the week. The leaders make use of members' experience to show how an individual can take responsibility for distinguishing between obligations and desires as an ongoing life task. In exploring their "wants," some clients will have begun to examine their emotional life more thoroughly and can be encouraged to continue this effort.

2. Evaluation of the workshop.

The leaders stimulate group discussion of the value of the techniques introduced in the workshop. Members are encouraged to discuss frankly their reactions to all of the techniques offered. It is expected that individuals will have had differing success with the variety of techniques practiced during the workshop. The group members are also encouraged to discuss their reactions to the leaders' style and behavior. One of the benefits of this discussion appears to be a differentiation of attitude toward the leaders and workshop, reducing the tendency toward idealization of the leaders with its attendant threat of collapse of the new behavior upon termination. Individual members may also use this discussion to explore their needs for additional assistance, an exploration often supported by other members, especially those who are engaged in counseling during the course of the workshop.

3.   Written evaluation.

Following the group discussion of the workshop, the leaders request that each member complete a written evaluation instrument. Upon completion (about 10–15 min.) arrangements are made to meet again as a group in four to six weeks.

SESSION 8

This follow-up meeting is not structured as the seven working sessions have been. The leaders adopt a less directive approach from the beginning. Members take the initiative for reacquaintance and for reporting on their progress during the previous weeks. The leader's role is to facilitate discussion and to obtain more refined judgments of the utility of different techniques for the members. These judgments can be used in further refinements of future workshops. Discussion and acceptance of individuals' experiences facilitates transition of responsibility to the individual and permits more effective referral when appropriate. The written evaluation instrument is administered a second time during this meeting.

Women Aware by The Staff of the Counseling and Student Development Center at Northern Illinois Univ.

Another theme group with a specific purpose and target population is the "Women Aware" program under the direction of Lu Ann Keating, which was designed by female faculty, staff, and students from several agencies at Northern Illinois University, De Kalb. This group aims at assisting women to increase self-understanding and self-awareness, with particular focus on being female and the ways in which femaleness influences the quality of their lives. The following sections describe the specific objectives and component activities of this structured theme group.

GROUP FORMAT.   The goal of this group is to increase participants' "female awareness." Program planners have defined female awareness to include the following:

1. our own perception of the female role has an impact on our behavior;
2. we *choose* how to define our femaleness whether we know it or not;
3. our definition of our female role has implications for our vocational choices, self-image, self-concept, and general awareness of our personal potential;
4. our culture stereotypes women, is prejudiced against women, and is ignorant about women, all of which have an effect on our self-image and our relationships with other women;
5. our socialization as women and our histories have to do with how we see ourselves now; and
6. our physical selves and our feelings about it have an effect on our behavior.

Based on these observations, a set of five participant objectives was identified, and two-hour small group sessions were designed to facilitate accomplishment of each objective. A typical group has from six to ten members, and, ideally, two cofacilitators. Session activities and objectives are summarized below.

SESSION 1

The objective of the initial meeting is to explore historical and cultural perceptions of femininity. The following activities are suggested for this session.

1.   Unfinished sentences (60 min.)

These may be passed out on mimeographed sheets or not, as the leaders decide. They may be written and then read or spoken aloud with only a short time allowed for answering. The best procedure is to go around the circle first without discussion since the participants may not be familiar with each other or each other's viewpoints yet. Notice that these sentences proceed from more general to more personal statements. Sometimes discussion and responding to some of the sentences may be saved for the end of the session; perhaps a contrast will be observed after the intervening activities change views.

1.   Today being a woman is_____ .
2.   A girl becomes a woman when _____ .
3.   Men expect women to be _____ .
4.   The women I like most always _____ .
5.   The women I like most never _____ .
6.   My mother is a lot more_____ than I am.
7.   I never wished I was a man until _____ .
8.   Unlike the average woman, I choose to _____ .
9.   As a woman, my potential may be _____ .
10. Because I'm a woman, I know I can _____ .

The following three exercises can be used separately or together as leaders wish for the rest of the session.

2.   Quotes (15–30 min.)

Below is a sampling of quotes from which leaders may choose several to read to the group and solicit brief reactions. Since the aim is to show that discrimination is historical and exists at the present time, even in statements from national leaders and persons thought to be quite radical, a wide variety can be included most effectively.

> Like most women (my wife) thinks with her glands instead of her head . . . When I got married I won my next election by 67,000 votes. So you can figure a good wife is worth at least 50,000 votes. (Senator Mark Hatfield, Oregon, 1973)

> We fully envision, however, that in the near future we will fly women into space and use them the same way we use them on earth—for the same purpose. (Astronaut James Lovell)

> But no one can evade the fact that in taking up a masculine calling, studying and working in a man's way, woman is doing something not wholly in agreement with, if not directly injurious to, her feminine nature. (Carl Jung, 20th century psychologist)

> Just get on with being woman, find the contentment and the reflected happiness of being secondary to men. (Wallace Reyburn, *The Inferior Sex*)

> Baseball is a contact sport. We have a five-page medical report which points out that girls are incapable of competing on the same level with boys. Their bones are more vulnerable, their reactions slower. (Robert Stirrat, Publicity Director of Little League)

> Whenever a woman dies there is one quarrel less on earth. (German proverb)

> There is a good principle which created order, light, and man, and an evil principle which created chaos, darkness, and woman. (Pythagoras)

> It would be preposterously naive to suggest that a B.A. degree can be made as attractive to girls as a marriage license. (Grayson Kirk, former president, Columbia University)

> The only alliance I would make with the Women's Libera-
> tion Movement is in bed. (Abbie Hoffman)

> Women on the average have more passivity in the inborn
> core of their personality. . . . I believe women are designed
> in their deeper instincts to get more pleasure out of life
> when they are not aggressive. (Taken from a quote by Benja-
> min M. Spock, *Decent and Indecent*)

Some more commonly heard statements from not-so-
notable voices include these, to be read aloud in run-on
sentence fashion.

> A woman's place is in the home. If you're so smart, why
> aren't you married? Can you type? A smart woman never
> shows her brains. Women are always playing hard to get.
> Don't worry your pretty little head about it. Dumb broad.
> Women like to be raped. A woman's work is never done. All
> you do is cook and clean and sit around all day. Women hate
> to be with other women. Women are always off chattering
> with each other. Some of my best friends are women . . .

3.   "Click!" (15–30 min.)

The leaders present the following stimulus materials
to the group:

The "click" phenomenon was first labeled by *Ms.* mag-
azine in its inaugural issue. The "click" experience happens when you are going along minding your own business
and suddenly something happens to make you realize that
women are considered inferior by our culture—or that *you,*
as a woman, are considered inferior in some way. You may
have seen the ad or heard the phrase or experienced the
event many times before—but, somehow, suddenly it hits
you in a new way—"click." Be careful of expressing your
new awareness of this. You may be accused of being over-
sensitive, or paranoid, or a "woman's libber"—but you
know, inside, that you felt that *click* and that you won't let
it go by again.

Here are some examples:

You suddenly notice that all the "remove hair perma-
nently" ads are directed toward women. Click! Why is it
okay for men to be hairy on their faces, arms, legs, and not
women? Why don't men want to "remove hair perma-
nently" instead of shaving every day? Next day it hits you
that almost all diet aid ads (Ayds, Kelp, and B-6 diet) are
directed toward women. Click! Aren't men ever overweight? Sure they are! So why aren't the ads directed toward the paunchy executive? How come, instead, a lot of
the exercise ads are for men? Could it be—click!—that it's
because in our culture youth and passive beauty are much
more important for women—because men say so? Why?
What? How come?

A female physician is standing around at a cocktail
party listening to people ask her husband, "And what do
you do?" Click! Why doesn't anyone ask her? Could it be
that they never considered that she might have an exciting
career?

Another woman whose day began at 6 a.m. is at the
same party. That day she got the kids up, fed them, dressed
them, got them off to school, cleaned the downstairs, went
shopping, had lunch ready, took the baby for a checkup,
cleaned the upstairs, carpooled the kids home, settled an
argument, found another babysitter at the last minute, had
her husband's suit ready, and charmed his boss at a party.
Someone says to her, "Let's see, Mrs. Smith, you're not
working, are you?" What do you call "work" anyway?

A boy who "acts like a girl" is a "sissy" while a girl who
"acts like a boy" is a "tomboy." To be a tomboy is some-

thing adults indulge and find cute; to be a sissy is something that alarms people. Click! Could it be that it's understandable why anyone would want to act like a boy, and not understandable why anyone would want to act like a girl—unless she happens to be one? Could it be that acting like a girl just isn't very admirable?

4. Labor statistics—their implications (15–30 min.)

A condensation of an article by Bem and Bem (1973) which draws on some U.S. Department of Labor statistical data to amplify further the discriminatory treatment of women—this time in the world of work is presented.

5. Unfinished sentences, a review (10–15 min.)

The group can turn again to the incomplete sentences used at the outset of the meeting and discuss any alterations in their responses to them, or possibly add new, more personal ones.

At the close of the first session, each member is given a copy of the Polly Williams story (fictional biographical sketch) for discussion at the beginning of the next meeting.

SESSION 2

The aim of this session's activities is to explore our own socialization as women.

1. Polly Williams Story (30–40 min.)

The leaders begin Session 2 with a full group discussion of the Polly Williams story assigned as homework by asking some of the following open-ended questions (or others of their own choice).

What was your reaction to reading about Polly Williams?
What do you think about Polly Williams?
Was Polly's life "just an ordinary life?"
How did you respond to Polly's "drifting" into womanhood?
How did you respond to her whole "drifting" life before marriage?

What were your reactions when Polly's drifting life turned toward a strict new orientation—the life of her husband and family?

2. Who's who for you? (45 min.)

The area of role models is looked at via "who's who for you?" For this activity, the leaders divide the members into two smaller groups for discussion. The items to be answered by each participant are:

a. Name three people you admire or respect.
b. Name three people who have had the greatest impact on your life.
c. What one person would you most like to be like?

Each member writes down on a sheet of paper her answers to the above questions. Then, in the two subgroups, each coleader moderates a discussion using the following questions to frame the interchange:

a. Whom did you list for each of the three questions? Why?
b. What is your relationship with these persons?
c. Are they male or female? Would your answers have been different if this had not been a female group?
d. What are the common characteristics you see in these people that you like?
e. Do you see those characteristics in yourself? If not, how are you planning to incorporate them?
f. Did you consider putting yourself as the person you'd most like to be like?

3. Parents' chat (30 min.)

The area of family influences and expectations can be

explored with this activity. The following instructions are given:

    a.   Pair up with someone and sit together. I want you each to imagine that you are your mother.

    b.   You and this other mother have just met and are each talking to the other about your daughter, i.e., yourself. In other words, you are talking about yourself as you imagine your mother might have talked about you at various times in your life.

    c.   First, take a few minutes to converse about the birth of your daughter, talking as your mother might have talked shortly after your own birth. Discuss your hopes and dreams for this new baby daughter. Are you glad she is a girl? What do you expect from her? Are these expectations different than they might have been had she been a boy?

Allow several minutes for each discussion, and then continue.

    d.   Now, take another few minutes to converse with the parent, this time talking to each other about your daughter as she is now—what she has done with her life, how you feel about her, whether she has met your expectations, how she compares with any other children you have, or whatever else occurs to you.

Allow another five minutes or so for such conversation. You may have the "mothers" mingle and chat with several other parents. When the conversation is stopped, have them break into groups of about five and give them the following directions:

    e.   Take several minutes to discuss what you have discovered through this experience. How did you feel about doing this? What did you learn about your mother? About yourself? Are you like your mother? If so, does that bother you? Do you think your mother likes you? Did she like you when you were little? Have you checked this out with her recently? What did you notice about the "mothers" of your partners?

SESSION 3

The objective here is to determine how our socialization affects us.
1. Saturday night at the dorm (45–60 min.)
To examine the role of peers and peer influence, this session begins with the following activity. Give each participant a list of the "dorm residents," as follows:

Peggy: does not really have any plans, so will use the evening for studying and watching TV by herself

Susan: gets together with other friends with no plans; they go out for the evening together

Jane: does not date a lot, but has a first date tonight with a guy in her math class

Karen: plans to spend the evening with a girl friend in another dorm

Mary: has few dates; tonight she's going out with a friend of her roommate's boy friend (whom she's never met)

Sally: has a steady boy friend and goes out almost every weekend—always seems to have a good time

Ann: has no plans here, so she went home for the weekend

Linda: has plans to be with several women friends, but broke the plans when she was asked out by a guy

Carol: has been looking forward all week to this free time so she could work on a project

The following questions for discussion are suggested, but others may be added. The leaders break the group into two subgroups to discuss these questions: (a) Which of these persons have you been? How did you feel in that situation? Why? (b) Have you felt social pressure in these situations? From men? Women? Yourself? (c) Which ones would you like to be? Why?

2.   Relationships with men (45–60 min.)

The previous activity leads readily into discussion of the area of heterosexual relationships. For this the participants move back into the full group. The leaders ask some of the following open-ended questions and/or add their own.

a.   Do you see your relationship with men (friends, boyfriends, father, relatives) as having influenced your ideas about yourself (as a woman)?

b.   Are you a different "self" (woman) in the company of men than you are with women?

c.   Do you act differently with men than with women? Do you play a different role?

d.   In what ways is the influence of men different from the influence of women?

e.   How have culture and society influenced your relationships with men and your ideas about yourself as a woman?

f.   Do you feel different about yourself after getting compliments from men on your attractiveness and/or appearance?

g.   How have you felt (about yourself) when you were not dating?

SESSION 4

In this meeting participants focus on dimensions of their physical being such as attractiveness, health, and sexuality, with a view toward understanding cultural influences on their attitudes and behavior. For these activities, the time frame can be altered, and some or all of the activities used at the leaders' discretion.

1. Body talk
a. Attractiveness and beauty (15 min.)

The group is divided into triads to complete the open-ended sentences below, with five minutes allowed for each sentence.

"The three things I would most like to change about my body are . . . "
"I think I am most attractive when . . ."
"The thing I like most about my body is . . ."

The leaders then ask participants if they found important similarities or important differences among their responses.

b. *Memoirs of an Ex-Prom Queen* (20 min.)

The leaders hand out copies of excerpted pages from Kate Shulman's (1972) book (suggested pages include excerpts from pp. 20–27). Reactions are discussed in the total group. How important is beauty to you? For whom do you wish to be beautiful? Do men worry about their looks as much as women? Are they judged on their looks as much as women? Who do you think is beautiful?

2. Health (20 min.)

The leaders begin by reading this statement. The preface is geared toward college students, but this information is useful to all.

Now that you are here at NIU—on your own, away from home—you have both the freedom and the responsibility of your own bodies. No one will tell you to eat more or less, no one will tell you to get more sleep, no one will know you have a sore throat and need to see a doctor—unless you tell them. You are responsible for your physical selves in a way you have not been before. Exercise, nutrition, birth control, yearly checkups—all are your health in the future. How does this way of looking at it strike you? Have you been feeling or acting responsible in this way? Are there experiences about this you'd like to share?

They then pass out the women's health fact sheet, with instructions to read and discuss selected facts in the total group. (The following facts are examples from a list of 20 items; others are easily constructed.)

Some Health Facts For Females That Should Be Common Knowledge But Are Not

1. The vaginal walls are self-cleansing tissue. Washing the external genitals with soap and water is all that is necessary for cleanliness. Douching, unless for medical purposes and prescribed by a physician, is not necessary.
2. Ditto for vaginal deodorant sprays, which are not only unnecessary but for many women are harmful. Imagine spraying those harsh chemicals on the tissue inside your mouth; the tissues are much the same. Don't let Madison Avenue fool you into thinking you need to buy these products.
3. Ordinarily, vaginal itching is *not* a symptom of V. D. It is usually a symptom of rather common vaginal infections (trichomonas or monilia) which can be treated quite easily. Don't suffer in silence!

4.   Any reducing diet which does not include foods from the "basic four" groups of foods—dairy, vegetable, grain, and high protein products—is lacking in essential nutrition. Don't let weight loss become health loss for you. Prolonged use of fad diets can cause malnutrition, hormonal imbalance, and assorted other unpleasant effects, including death.

5.   There are birth control methods available at low cost without prescription which are almost as effective as the pill—a condom and contraceptive foam used together. (But use them correctly!) Buy them at any drugstore. Remember, if you and your partner don't communicate well enough to talk about preventing pregnancy, you don't really communicate well enough to make love.

6.   Every female over 17 needs a yearly Pap smear for cervical cancer. It is absolutely painless and should be part of a routine pelvic examination.

7.   Many college students experience emotional difficulty during their college years. For the only time in your life, confidential help in counseling is available for you at no cost. Don't minimize your distress and don't let false pride get in the way of admitting to yourself that you could use an objective listener.

8.   Both treatments for V. D. (penicillin) and trichomonas (Flagyl) should never be mixed with alcohol. Alcohol reduces the effectiveness of penicillin, and, with Flagyl, can make you very sick.

9.   If for any reason you are taking tranquilizers or barbiturates, never consume alcohol with them. These drugs can combine with alcohol to produce an effect many times stronger than either

would produce separately—an effect that can be lethal.

10.   If you are raped or assaulted, do not go home, do not go shower, but go straight to a hospital or health service, get treated, get confirmation of your injuries, and then, please file a complaint with the police so that this experience doesn't happen to someone else.

11.   Hypertension hits people of all ages, and *has no symptoms.* (Having a hot temper, being tense, or have a red face are *not* symptoms of hypertension). This can be checked painlessly with a blood pressure check. Make sure it's a part of your yearly physical.

12.   If you have been smoking for less than five years, and quit now, your lungs will be almost back to normal in ten years.

13.   Yes, there are alcoholics your age. Plenty of them. Major clues to a drinking problem are: drinking alone, drinking *in order to* have a good time or relax, not feeling free to turn down a drink, and not being able to remember events that happened while drinking. Realize, please, that alcohol abuse hits all kinds of people and that it doesn't help to fool yourself if you do suspect a problem. Get help!

14.   Regular exercise should be a part of everyone's life, not just for figure and weight control, but for heart-lung efficiency. Developing a daily program of running, bicycling, swimming, or even walking fast can pay off in later years as well as now.

3.   Sexuality (remainder of session)

The leaders hand out the following excerpt from *Sexuality* by Peg Mayo, which is reprinted from the University of South Dakota *Crisis Intervention Resource Manual* (1973).

If I do not know that you will love me tomorrow, dare I love
you today, uncertain as I am of my attractiveness and my
courage? Dare I turn you away? Will a chance ever come
again? What choices do I make on what standards? Do I turn
you away because I have vowed virginity to my dreamed-of-
husband-to-be, or do I turn you away because I am afraid my
vulva is deformed (I haven't found a good illustration in a
book yet), or do I turn you away because you are not hand-
some enough for me to brag about, or do I turn you away
because I am certain I will be physically hurt, or do I accept
you because you are wanted by others, or do I accept you
because my body responds to your body, or, finally, do I
accept you because I love you? Do I insist that I accept you
spontaneously and thereby forget whatever I know of birth
control? Do I plan for you to come to my house when my
parents are away, knowing there is danger they will return?
Do I find your body miraculous or hideous? Do I flaunt mine
or hide it? How do *you* feel about all this . . . do you even
think to wonder? Am I ashamed or proud or pleased or
betrayed or satisfied or hurt or delighted or comforted on
the winner? Who am I? A young woman in this case.

Following their reading of this, the group can engage
in open discussion of their reactions to it. If the discussion
lags, these incomplete sentences can be shared with the
group, and their individual responses to them solicited and
discussed.

1. To me, the sexual revolution means . . .
2. The thing that confuses me most about sex is . . .
3. I disapprove of . . .
4. Love and sex . . .

SESSION 5

The overall objective for this last meeting is to help
group participants to focus on future life style choices.
1. Relaxation and fantasy exercise (10 min.)
The leader may want to add to the following introduction and tie in personal insights gained over the previous
sessions:

"In this, our final session, we'll explore some of our fantasies, needs, personal goals, and possible careers. Before we let our fantasies loose, let's relax our bodies and minds, and remove present distractions."

In a soothing tone, the leader gives suggestions for physical relaxation, e.g., "Close your eyes, get in a comfortable position," etc. (leader adds her own relaxation patter). Then, she should say, "Think back about all the hope you had for the future as a child, what career you once thought of, what needs you had in following up on those choices, how you've pursued those goals to date, and what decisions you've made to arrive here."

2. Career exploration (10–15 min.)

The members are divided into two smaller groups, and each woman describes what she would like to do with her life, and how that would fulfill certain needs and interests. Each may want to describe her previous fantasy to accomplish this.

3. Personal objectives and strategies (20–30 min.)

Each participant is given a sheet of paper on which she is instructed to write some personal objectives and specific strategies for working toward each of them. The leader should encourage the group members to describe at least one simple, short-range objective and one long-range one. After allowing about ten minutes for filling out the individual sheets, the members form two small groups and share a discussion of their personal objectives.

4. On focus (30 min.)

This exercise has proven to be the most useful and appealing one in this session. In it, each member is given a turn to sit in the "focus" spot. All other members then select for the focus person a top job they could imagine that person achieving sometime in the future and one job they believe would *not* meet the personal needs of the focus person. Discussion of those selected jobs is delayed until the round is completed for each person. The purposes of this activity are twofold, namely, to expand one's awareness of personal careers and activities which might satisfy needs, and to give and receive feedback.

Following completion of this exercise, the leaders should summarize the learnings, and, after soliciting both brief verbal and written evaluation of the individual sessions and the program as a whole, adjourn the group.

SUMMARY

This chapter has focused on another category of structured groups called "life theme groups," which deal with intrapersonal issues vital to living a satisfying life and setting and achieving meaningful goals. The six programs described were chosen because of their completeness, variety of focus, and developmental import. The following chapter describes a third category of structured groups, those concerned with "life transitions." The major objective of these group programs is to help persons cope with significant and traumatic major changes in their lives that occur suddenly, without planning, or that are undertaken consciously and by design. Three life transition groups are described therein.

Chapter 5

LIFE TRANSITION GROUPS

This third category of structured developmental groups has as its central objective the learning of behaviors that will be effective in coping with major changes in life. These changes include those sudden, unanticipated occurrences that seem to "happen to us" as well as those changes that are more self-intentioned and volitional. More specifically, transition groups are structured to help people cope with changes like the loss of a mate or significant others through death, divorce, or separation, or other major transitions like relocation, physical impairment, or loss of employment.

Studies over the past ten years of stress-generating life events (Holmes & Rahe, 1967; Masuda & Holmes, 1967; Rahe et al., 1970; Paykel et al., 1969, 1971; Aakster, 1974) have reported on the nature and consequences of individuals' ill-preparedness to handle them. These studies point up the importance of providing resources to help people deal with critical periods of change, particularly in light of the absence of any rituals or systematic means for completing those transitions with a minimum of disability. The majority of major life changes—at least in American society —appear to be unanticipated, despite their predictability. Too often, lack of preparation or refusal to recognize signs of impending change, render people incapable of making the necessary adaptations or coping successfully with the consequences of the upheaval.

FOCUS OF LIFE TRANSITION GROUPS

The aforementioned studies detail a list of events that are most stress producing. As mentioned in Chapter 1, these appear to be mostly of three types, that is, change due to death, change in a significant personal and social relationship, and changes which have gravely unfavorable economic consequences.

The structure of transition groups varies widely, and thus there are fewer core components or format similarities. Fewer examples of this type of structured group have been developed to date than of either life skills or life theme groups. Life transition groups offer possibilities for achieving personal adjustment that range from a somewhat regimented series of exercises to little more structure than one typically finds in an open-ended personal growth group. In the latter case, the only structure may be possession of a common, identifiable, openly shared transition-goal statement and adoption of some time-limiting parameters for the duration of the group.

Life transition groups have been devised for a number of major life changes. Representative titles among them include, "Resolving Personal Loss," "Leaving the Nest," "Transition Group for Separated and Divorced Persons," "Coping with Change," "Women Alone," and "Search for Fulfillment." Practically all share the emphasis on assisting persons in interpersonal relationship transitions. As with all developmental structured groups, the dual intent is to help individuals meet their immediate need for the resolution of problems and at the same time learn a coping style that will serve them in future similar situations.

DESCRIPTION OF LIFE TRANSITION GROUPS

The next part of this chapter describes several representative life transition groups chosen for their completeness and diversity of focus. Like life transition groups, they are presented in narrative style rather than in outline format, as their structure is less formal than that of the life skills groups described in Chapter 3.

Transition Group for Separated and Divorced Persons by James D. Morris and Mary R. Prescott

The following program is designed to help individuals cope with the adjustment demands of postpartnership following separation or divorce. It was designed by James D. Morris of the University of Idaho Counseling Center in Moscow, Idaho, and Mary R. Prescott, currently of the Department of Counseling and Educational Psychology at New Mexico State University in Las Cruces. Their description of this life transition group follows.

This group experience was designed to deal with the changes involved in an individual's returning to single life while still making adjustments to the dissolution of the former partnership. It provides a supportive vehicle for sharing strengths and exploring concerns by separated and divorced persons.

GROUP FORMAT   Experience with this program over the past three years has shown it to be most desirable to have a male-female facilitator team. Such an arrangement enables the often stereotyped thinking which some expartners generalize to all members of the opposite sex to be confronted and worked through more satisfactorily. An approximately equal sex distribution among participants is also desirable, with a total membership of between seven and twelve. The current model involves nine weekly sessions of two hours each.

All applicants are screened in an interview with one of the coleaders. Exclusion from the group is usually based on serious therapeutic need, with persons exhibiting extreme neuroticism or pathology being referred for individual assistance. During the screening interview several of the ground rules are also discussed. These typically include brief explanations of the group process and specific prohibitions against dating other members for the duration of the group.

The program is advertised using the campus media and posters or flyers. These notices focus on the concerns of separated or divorced persons and the importance of supportive sharing and therapeutic problem solving.

Unlike many programs of a similar nature, this kind of transition group uses no specific exercises or games, or a preplanned format. The sessions are unstructured, and, as most members come to the group eager to discuss their concerns, no contrivance is needed to initiate discussion. The first session is used for repeating ground rules, setting a tone for participation, and sharing expectations for outcomes.

While there is no organized sequence of learning experiences, the authors have noted a pattern of three somewhat distinct states through which the group moves. This flow is perhaps best characterized by a change in the participants' time perspective. Initially, the focus is on the past relationship, its attendant characteristics, and the resultant feelings of loneliness, guilt, anger, bitterness, resentment, or relief. The first phase could be labeled the "mourning" period, and a thorough exploration of such feelings by each individual consumes the largest portion of the group experience, coming to a close usually in five or six sessions. Gains from this phase include realization that others share similar experiences and reactions, and awareness of the various ways of coping used by different members. A major related outcome of this period is for people to understand the ups and downs experienced in the relationship, and to appreciate the demise of the relationship and their role in it. Honest feedback and group cohesion come to characterize these groups early in their existence, and provide the climate for participants to examine openly the components that led to the deterioration of the partnership.

A second stage seems to occur between sessions six and eight wherein the concern shifts to the present and "here-and-now" matters. During this time, participants usually begin to understand more fully their "unattached" roles and the needs they have as single persons. Part of the group's function at this time is to support each individual's attempts to restructure his/her life style and intrapersonal framework. A major part of that function is accomplished through clarification of values and goals.

A third and final phase occurs when participants begin to shift to a future perspective. In this period group members earnestly move into personal goal setting in light of their reassessed self-images. Greater insight and self-confidence are notable in this latter stage of group life, as the group solidifies in its support of each member's plans and life style preferences. At this point, participants are usually ready to move ahead on their own, and the group terminates. Occasionally persons sign up for a second group.

The Personal Orientation Inventory, administered immediately before and after the group experience, has been used as a measure of change. Results have shown significant change in desirable directions.

The consumers of this particular program appear to be atypical of the usual campus counseling agency clientele. The average age is around thirty, and about the same numbers of males and females enroll. To date, divorced individuals are in the majority, although a substantial number of persons who have broken off a cohabitation relationship apply, as do students who are separated from their marriage partners.

Resolving Personal Loss by Eugene Knott

Another life transition group has been designed to facilitate adjustment to the loss of a significant relationship due to death. This particular program was devised by Eugene Knott of the Counseling Center at the University of Rhode Island, Kingston.

GROUP FORMAT.   The general objectives of this group are to assist bereaved individuals with recognition of their loss, to further necessary grief work in a supportive climate, and to create a socially acceptable mourning rite by helping individuals to discuss openly the death of a loved one. The desired ultimate outcome is to offer emotional catharsis to bereaved persons, and to help them begin the process of resuming their normal lives with the mutual support of similarly fated "victims."

The group is usually restricted to six to eight participants, and a screening interview is held with each prospective member. Persons are accepted who recently lost someone close to them. In most cases, family members of the deceased and other close loved ones seem to be ready for such a group experience three to four weeks after the death. Persons with less intimate ties are able to benefit from the group experience sooner after the death. In any event, it is suggested that persons of greatly varying intensity of loss not be placed in the same group. The ability to acknowledge one's grief actively and publicly, called mourning, is essential to the grief resolution process, and may not be immediately possible for persons suffering a deeply significant loss. The present pattern calls for five weekly sessions of two hours each, with each session devoted to a specific topic. Each of the topics is germane to the needs commonly demonstrated by bereaved persons, including those situations where a "retarded" grief reaction is involved. To date, a majority of participants have come to the group after passage of a substantial period of time since the death loss, usually six months or more.

SESSION 1

Opening activities involve introducing members by name to each other, and having them share, first in dyads, then with the total group, their responses to "Why I'm here," "What I hope to gain," and "Who has died." This part of the session has several related purposes, that is, (1) to enable members to begin "accommodating" themselves to each other (a sort of warmup); (2) to help members begin to see themselves as "acceptable" persons and members of a group consisting of folks with similar needs and similar experiences; and (3) to begin to establish an atmosphere that is essentially nonthreatening.

Although the second part of this first session can precede the first, recent experience would indicate that it is more satisfying when the leader's presentation is held till after the ice has been broken.

In the latter half of Session 1, the group leader explains (from his/her perspective) the goals of the group, and provides an overview of the five sessions. She/he states the expectations for both leaders and members, and offers some commentary covering the types of changes members might expect for themselves. The members are encouraged to share their feelings as candidly as comfort allows and to discuss the impact of their death loss. Unlike many other group experiences, they are also encouraged to talk about their feelings between sessions with nonmembers, particularly others who knew the dead person. Such objectives as "grief shared is grief diminished," and giving "permission" to detach oneself from all but the memory of the dead are facilitated in this manner. In the first meeting then, these issues are openly discussed.

SESSION 2

The leader begins this session by speaking briefly of some of the most typical reactions of persons bereaved by the death of someone cherished. This can be effectively accomplished by asking each member to react briefly to such experiences as feelings of loneliness, reactions of anger and guilt, the consequences of stigma (social treatment of bereaved by uneasy sympathizers) and deprivation, and, finally, the notion of transition itself, including the goals of detachment and reintegration—prime goals for each individual within the group. Other typical topics for discussion may include both somatic reactions and economic situations consequent to the loss.

Through this activity group members are given the opportunity to identify their primary grief reactions and to begin to "own" them. Thus, the objectives are several: (1) for members immediately to see the "legitimacy" and commonness of having such emotional responses to their death loss; (2) to provide the leader (and group) with a picture of the range and intensity of these issues for this particular group (they usually vary somewhat); and (3) to gain information so that this and the next two sessions can be organized about the more demanding concerns of the members.

This is a good point at which to give members some "homework," beginning with an exchange of phone numbers among those who desire. The purpose is to enable them to "check" with each other between sessions. All too often the recently bereaved undergo "leper-like" social treatment by people normally close to them, and the concern demonstrated by one person's merely attending to another with as little as a periodic phone call can be a powerful element in helping to resolve grief. This is especially useful when death is relatively recent, and even more so if the death resulted in someone's being widowed.

SESSION 3

This meeting is begun with a general inquiry about the "homework," members' contacts since the last session, and any notable occurrences a group member may wish to share. Following that, the leader focuses attention on a topic uncovered in the previous session's debriefing. It seems that "anger" and "guilt" feelings are most often the dominant concerns at this juncture of the group's life. In talking openly about such conflicting and (to them) supposedly inimical feelings, members ventilate their feelings and hopefully gain some perspective on understanding them.

The last portion of this third meeting is devoted to a lecturette by the leader on "normal grief reactions," and on time as a key variable in the mourning process. Material for this can be drawn from the work of Lindemann (1944), Bowlby (1961), and Parkes (1972). Often issues such as the quandary of keeping up with the daily demands of living in the face of immobilizing depression, the ambiguity of the future, and strained or absent social activity, are teased out and discussed at some length in this session. All of this discussion obviously is intended to help bereaved members to cope with their grief.

SESSION 4

During this session, the focus is on "stigma" and the social distance and relative isolation that the death of a person confers on anguished survivors. Also, the effects of "deprivation"—both social and economic—usually come to the fore. Personal fears of vulnerability and mortality, especially such fears as "cancer contagion" or hereditary defects, should also be dealt with openly in this meeting if they have not surfaced before. These are common, yet will vary from group to group.

In this session, and to a lesser extent in the previous one, the leader may find it useful to employ some "rational contradiction." Disputation of seemingly irrational fears, while not always consoling, will usually make an impact on a bereaved person over time.

This is also the session in which the group begins to "bridge the gap" from being centered on the past (dead) to focusing on the present (the living self and others), and ultimately to planning for the future. One way to facilitate this transition is to use a device like the Gestalt "empty chair" technique for "saying goodbye" to the dead person(s). This has the purpose of helping members to confirm (aloud) the death and absence, and thereby gain some semblance of psychological "closure" on that episode.

A typical homework assignment for the final session requires members to return the following week with some well-considered strategies for dealing with their day-to-day needs and wants in light of the major changes incurred by the death loss. It has proved helpful to encourage members to write down these strategies and share their notes at the next meeting.

SESSION 5

To begin this final meeting, members form groups of two to four persons each, the exact composition to be of their own choosing. Within these small groups, each individual shares his/her plans, with the other member(s) offering supportive critique, suggestions, and encouragement.

About two-thirds of the way through the session, the leader reconvenes the total group and solicits voluntary reactions to the discussions held in the subgroups. After briefly processing those, the leader then recapitulates the progress of the group, eliciting members' comments along the way. She/he then urges individuals to recognize and affirm their change and progress to date and their new ability to adjust to life in the face of death, and to note other gains made in the course of the five weeks, including new friends and resources.

Finally, the predictable matter of separation anxiety needs to be dealt with. It has been found useful to respond to this need by asking each member to speak briefly about what the group has meant to her/him, citing specific personal highlights. This activity concludes the group experience. The objectives of this session are to make the transition from *group* to *self* as "major resource" in the grieving process, and to enable participants to affirm their directions and goals for "satisfactory survival."

With a target behavior like the process of grieving, there are several options of which the leader should be cognizant throughout. The five-session format just outlined, for example, is most useful with persons who are dealing with the death of a family member. However, the general format and many of the specific activities can be used with other types of death loss. With such incidents as campus suicide or homicide, for example, a modification of this format has been used successfully. In such cases, the students living in close proximity to the dead victim become the target group. Adaptations suitable for their needs include initiation of the group very soon after the incident, and special emphasis on feelings of guilt and personal vulnerability—typically of paramount concern in such situations. Feedback from group members—both during the final meeting and at unsolicited times in later weeks and months—indicates that this structured group experience provides helpful resolution of a number of feelings for the bereaved.

Women Alone by Susan Hofmann and Floyd C. Kennedy

Transition groups frequently focus on very specific target populations with equally precise characteristics. One such program is entitled "Women Alone," which was devised by Susan Hofmann and Floyd C. Kennedy of the Counseling and Career Development Center at Metropolitan State College in Denver, Colorado. Participation in this group is limited to women who previously have shared life with a man (married or unmarried) but no longer are in such a relationship, and to single women who have children and may or may not have had such a sharing relationship. Their description of the elements and course of this program follows.

GROUP FORMAT.   The group is led by a male and female team of facilitators and has from eight to ten members.

We meet for nine weekly sessions of two hours each; a small, comfortable room provides an ideal setting. The following set of objectives is shared individually with group members prior to the initial meeting.

1. To provide an understanding and supportive group climate within which each participant may reassess her total life situation (i.e., present circumstances, goals, values, feelings about self, feelings about others, etc.).
2. To provide realistic consultation from both the professional and the lay point of view.
3. To share with others in similar circumstances one's own experience and to learn from the experience of others.

4. To provide emotional and intellectual support (i.e., acceptance and reassurance) during this difficult period of her life.

5. To assist mothers without mates to handle the difficult task of rearing children alone.

6. To help the "woman alone" to come to grips with the reality that she is alone and may be alone for a significant period of her life.

7. Within this emotionally secure environment, to help each participant to bring about changes in her life style that potentially will lead to a more satisfying life.

Prospective group members are also told that we expect to achieve these objectives by: (1) intensive discussion at group meetings of the topics given later (plus other topics suggested by group members); (2) role playing and group exercises; and (3) well thought out changes that each participant will be expected to begin to make in her real life situation.

SESSION 1

In the first meeting, we begin with an open-ended discussion in which group members (and leaders) share why they have sought this group experience, and what they personally hope to accomplish. This is followed by a discussion of some general group guidelines, the leaders providing a stimulus for this by handing out a brief, one-page statement which outlines some common norms for a counseling group.

Once these preliminaries are dealt with, the group starts the first exercise. The objectives of this activity are to enable group members to get to know each other, and to give them a chance to talk briefly about themselves without interruption. The procedure involves three steps:

1. Each group member is asked to talk about her-self for five minutes, with an emphasis on "Who I am", and "How I see myself now."
2. After each group member speaks, other group members are asked to react to what has been said.
3. Discussion of similarities and differences in con-cerns is encouraged among the total group.

Finally, the leaders assign homework, asking each par-ticipant to give some lengthy thought to how she wants to use the group experience over the next eight weeks and to report back on this. Members are also instructed to peruse the following list of possible discussion topics and to iden-tify their concerns of personal value and priority from among them for sharing in the next meeting.

Discussion Topics

1. Feelings about one's self. Self-concept. Do you like you? Do you dislike you? What is good, bad, right, wrong with you? Are these your views? Or someone else's views? What changes would you like to make?
2. So you are now alone—with or without your chil-dren. What does this mean to you? What are your feelings about being alone? Are these feel-ings and thoughts helpful or hurtful? Should they be changed? Is it acceptable to be selfish?
3. What do you have going for you? What abilities, talents, skills do you have? What have been your achievements and successes? In what roles do you see yourself?
4. Are you more dependent than independent? Are you in control of your life? If not, what must you

do to gain control? Coping (just making do) vs. self-determination and growth? Decision making?

5. Do you work to help support yourself? If not, why not? Are these reasons realistic? Or, are they a "cop-out?" Could you get a job if you tried?

6. What short- and long-term goals do you have for yourself? If you have no well-defined goals, why not? If you do have well-defined goals, what are you doing about them?

7. Making changes in one's life-style is risky, but change in your life probably is mandatory. What changes must you make? How much risk can you tolerate? Work, living arrangements, etc.

8. How do you deal with feelings of loneliness, depression, guilt, rejection, anger, etc.?

9. Friends, exfriends, new friends. Love, sex, and the woman alone. Relations with the ex. Loving and being loved.

10. You and your children—expectations, satisfactions, frustrations, etc.

11. Marriage—remarriage. "I must have a man," fact or fiction?

12. Dealing with the new you and your new life.

SESSION 2

This session begins with sharing of responses to the homework assignments. Based on these reported concerns, the leaders make a list before the third session of tentative discussion topics for the next six meetings.

The remainder of this meeting is devoted to having the group members react to the following questions and discuss their responses. The particular objective of each of these questions is listed in parenthesis after each one.

1. Do you like yourself? (Used to encourage exploration of self-concept.)
2. How do you see yourself? What words do you
   use to describe yourself? (To enable members to
   recognize how they get to feeling the way they
   do.)
3. How do you think others see you? What differences do you see between questions 2 and 3? (To
   recognize the differences between internal and
   external messages relating to self.)
4. How do you see other members of this group?
   (To practice giving and receiving feedback.)

SESSIONS 3–8

For most of the group's remaining meetings the following format is employed: Each meeting begins first with
a brief report by each group member of her current feelings, and the relevant issues that are most pressing for
her, followed by group discussion of a new area of concern.

The set of members' topical concerns provides the
focal point for discussion in the next six meetings. Although these concerns will obviously vary from one group
to another, the general flow of topics is typically as follows.

1. The individual members' self-image, its components and sources.
2. Various aspects of living alone, use of time, relative dependence, loneliness, etc.
3. Dealing with "bad" feelings, such as depression,
   anxiety, guilt, worthlessness, stressful situations.
4. Relationships, dating, sex, remarriage.
5. Child rearing as a woman alone.
6. Change and decision making in our lives.

Throughout these sessions, the group monitors its own process with guidance from the leaders. This guidance includes feedback about individual members and their interactions, as well as an assessment of how the program is proceeding. A major part of the group's activities during these six sessions also consists of assigning several appropriate behavioral tasks. Examples of these assignments include "behavioral rehearsal" tasks, such as initiating conversations with new and different people, inviting someone to dinner, practicing more satisfying ways of relating to children—particularly regarding dating and other adult relationships—and goal setting with regard to resolution of practical economic matters like finances.

SESSION 9

In this final meeting, which serves as a wrap-up session, two main topics are addressed. First, the group takes a look at what steps each of the members can and should take from this point. Following that, a brief period is given over to evaluating the program via group discussion and completion of a short series of evaluation questions. These questions involve subjective responses from the members relative to the group experience as a whole, to the leaders, and to suggest revisions in format based on perceived gains for themselves.

SUMMARY

In this chapter, three life transition groups have been described, all developed to help persons deal with the upheaval resulting from major changes within their lives. In the final chapter, a summary of the book's goals and purposes, and the aims of the structured group approach are reviewed. It concludes with a look to the future for the structured group movement.

Chapter 6

SUMMARY AND FUTURE
DIRECTIONS

Summary

In this book, we have attempted to present an in-depth look at what has come to be a significant, widespread mental health intervention, that is, structured groups for facilitating development. These programs are essentially short-term, organized methods for aiding development in two main ways: first, they provide a means for remedying a particular skill deficiency or repairing a psychologically disabling experience; second, they enable helping agents to intervene preventively. In the latter case, the developmental needs that commonly emerge throughout the life span can be anticipated and dealt with. In other words, one need not depend on the elaboration of symptoms to address a client's needs. As Caplan and Grunebaum (1967) noted, this type of primary prevention has the potential for substantially counteracting the harmful influences that, over the long haul, produce emotional dysfunction in the population at risk.

These group approaches have several additional advantages. Primary among them is the two-pronged nature of the help offered whereby an individual can find the solution to a particular problem and, simultaneously, develop the skill or ability to resolve similar future quandaries. The general format of the groups optimizes time by limiting the number of sessions and by providing a learning forum for several persons at the same time. Structured groups employ a variety of methodologies and reflect well two currently valued dimensions of counseling services, proactivity and accountability. In many ways, the structured developmental group movement incorporates several of the plus factors and few of the weaknesses of the various movements which forged its genesis.

A conceptual schema has been employed to categorize generally the varying character of the different groups; three main categories of groups are differentiated: (1) life skills groups, which help members to acquire the skills necessary to cope effectively with daily interpersonal transactions; (2) life theme groups, which assist persons to resolve critical intrapersonal issues; and (3) life transition groups, which help individuals to adjust to major life changes. Ideally, successful learnings in both life skills and life theme areas equip individuals to handle necessary life transitions successfully. All three types of groups are goal directed and time limited. The establishment of specific goals within a predetermined time frame helps to make these types of interventions highly accountable strategies that become a viable alternative to so-called "talking" therapies.

The elements of structured developmental groups have been outlined, including consideration of pregroup variables, format, and evaluation. Within each type of structured group, a range of approaches has also been identified, with illustrations of several exemplary programs in each category. Within the life skills groups were included Anxiety Management Training, Assertive Behavior, Communication Skills Workshop, Couples Enrichment Workshop, Decision-Making, PATH, Friendship Initiation & Development, More Effective Parenting Program, and Profile Group for Weight Control. Representative life theme groups included Clarifying Personal Values, Human Sexuality, Loneliness and Self-Betrayal Workshop, Raising The Male Consciousness, Self-Esteem Workshop, and a program entitled Women Aware. Lastly, examples of life transition groups were the Transition Group for Separated and Divorced Persons, Resolving Personal Loss, and Women Alone program. A variety of structured developmental groups is continually under development, and the above can thus be considered a representative rather than an exhaustive list. It is hoped, in addition, that from reading this book, practitioners will be able to expand from the descriptions presented and design and develop their own locally relevant structured groups.

FUTURE DIRECTIONS

Anticipating directions which the burgeoning structured group movement will take in the future is perhaps best done by extrapolating from the present. Many of these types of programs are already incorporated into the formal school curriculum at various levels. Some have been expanded into full-term courses and are being offered for credit in colleges and universities. Still other examples can be found in middle and secondary schools where they frequently appear as mini-courses. Then, too, entire programs have evolved in recent years which integrate deliberate psychological or affective education approaches throughout the curriculum. In addition, groups of the type described herein are becoming more frequently offered in community agencies. As the value of this alternate mode of helping is realized by more mental health personnel, it seems reasonable to expect that structured developmental groups will become a widely employed therapeutic strategy throughout the helping professions. Current professional involvement in this area reflects the high level of consumer response to programs of this type, and each has, in its turn, become the impetus for expansion of the other.

However, as with many of the helping interventions, evaluation and empirical research lag behind the practice. A notable exception to this situation is found with life skills groups, wherein a reasonable amount of research data has been amassed in recent years. Needless to say, evaluation of all of these programs needs more consistent and sophisticated attention.

A survey of the entire movement at this time reveals a goal emerging relative to future application of structured developmental groups. We are already enmeshed in "playing catch-up." Because of heightening client interest, we can readily anticipate increased demand for programs like these at all levels of adolescent education, reaching over into adulthood. Our objective then is to seek implementation of these kinds of groups at earlier points in human development than is the case at present.

It has been stated that consumer response to these forms of intervention has already begun to foster momentum for growth of this movement. Although no single intervention mode will ever suffice universally, structured groups for facilitating development are increasingly becoming major tools in the mental health professional's repertoire of therapeutic and educational approaches to developmental change.

List of Contributors

The following is a list of program contributors and their complete mailing addresses.

Life Skills

Anxiety Management Training

Barry McCarthy
Department of Psychology
The American University
Massachusetts and Nebraska Avenues
Washington, D.C.

Assertion Training

Dolph Printz
Office of Counseling and Student Development
University of Rhode Island
Kingston, Rhode Island

Communication Skills Workshop

University Counseling Center
Colorado State University
Fort Collins, Colorado

Couples Enrichment Workshop

Richard Blouch
Counseling Center
Millersville State College
Lancaster, Pennsylvania

Decision-Making

Si Clifton and Robert Nejedlo
Student Development Center
Northern Illinois University
DeKalb, Illinois

Path

Howard Figler
Counseling Center
Dickinson College
Carlisle, Pennsylvania

Friendship Initiating and Development Group

Michale C. Menefee
Counseling and Psychological Services Center
The University of Texas at Austin
Austin, Texas

Parenting Skills Group

Lester Pearlstein
Counseling Center
University of Virginia
Charlottesville, Virginia

Joel Lipson
Department of Psychology
University of Wisconsin
Milwaukee, Wisconsin

Profile Group for Weight Control

Robert B. Mandell
Coordinator of Health and Counseling
The University of Texas at Dallas
Richardson, Texas

Life Themes

Clarifying Personal Values

Judy A. Marsh
20 Partridge St.
Portsmouth, New Hampshire

Human Sexuality

William H. Jones
Office of Counseling Services
Gettysburg College
Gettysburg, Pennsylvania

Loneliness and Self-Betrayal

Victor Atyas
Office of Counseling and Student Development
University of Rhode Island
Kingston, Rhode Island

Raising the Male Consciousness

Richard C. Nelson
Allen E. Segrist
Counseling and Personnel Services
Department of Education
Purdue University
West Lafayette, Indiana

Self-Esteem

Stanley Pavey
1551 North Murray Dr.
Los Angeles, California

Stanley Hunt
Counseling Center
University of Maryland
College Park, Maryland

Women Aware

Lu Ann Keating
Student Development Center
Northern Illinois University
DeKalb, Illinois

Life Transitions

Transition Group for Separated and Divorced Persons

James D. Morris
Student Counseling Center
University of Idaho
Moscow, Idaho

Mary R. Prescott
Department of Counseling and Educational Psychology
New Mexico State University
Las Cruces, New Mexico

Resolving Personal Loss

J. Eugene Knott
Office of Counseling and Student Development
University of Rhode Island
Kingston, Rhode Island

Women Alone

Susan Hofmann
Floyd C. Kennedy
Counseling and Career Development Center
Metropolitan State College
Denver, Colorado

REFERENCES

Aakster, C. Psycho-social stress and health disturbances. *Social Science and Medicine*, 1974, *8*, 77–90.

Adams, J., & Goldstein, M. J. A further study of coping style and behavioral response to stress. *Personality*, 1970, *1*, 231–141.

Alschuler, A. S. (Ed.). *New directions in psychological education*. Middletown, Conn.: Education Ventures, 1973.

Aries, P. The family, prison of love. *Psychology Today*, 1975, *9*, 52–58.

Bandura, A. *Principles of behavior modification*. New York: Holt, Rinehart and Winston, 1969.

Bandura, A. & Perloff, B. Relative efficacy of self-monitored and externally imposed reinforcement systems. *Journal of Personality and Social Psychology*, 1967, *7*, 111–116.

Bem, S. L. Androgyny vs. the tight little lives of fluffy women and chesty men. *Psychology Today*, 1975 (September), *9*, 58–62.

Bem, S. L., & Bem, D. F. *Training the woman to know her place*. Palo Alto, Calif.: Stanford University Press, 1973.

Bessell, H., & Palomares, U. *Methods in human development theory manual*. San Diego, Calif.: Human Development Training Institute, 1970.

Borton, T. *Reach, touch, and teach: Student concerns and process education*. New York: McGraw-Hill, 1970.

Bowlby, J. Processes of mourning. *International Journal of Psycho-Analysis*, 1961, *44*, 317–340.

Brown, G. *Human teaching for human learning: An introduction to confluent education*. New York: Viking, 1971.

Caplan, G., & Grunebaum, H. Perspectives on primary prevention: A review. *Archives of General Psychiatry*, 1967, *17*, 331–345.

Castillo, G. *Left-handed teaching: Lessons in affective education*. New York: Praeger, 1974.

Colley, S. Personal education. *Personnel and Guidance Journal*, 1975, *53*, 610–614.

Communication Skills Workshop Manual. University Counseling Center, Colorado State University, Fort Collins, Colorado, 1972.

Cudney, M. R. *Eliminating self-defeating behaviors*. Kalamazoo, Mich.: Life-Giving Enterprises, 1975.

Erikson, E. H. *Identity: Youth and crisis*. New York: Norton, 1968.

Figler, H. E. *PATH: A career workbook for liberal arts students*. Cranston, R.I.: Carroll Press, 1975.

Gelatt, H. B., et al. *Decisions and outcomes*. Princeton, New Jersey: College Entrance Examination Board, 1973.

Ginott, H. G. *Between parent and child*. New York: Macmillan, 1965.

Goldiamond, I. Self-control procedures in personal behavior problems. *Psychological Reports*, 1965, *17*, 851–868.

Gordon, T. *Parent effectiveness training.* New York: Wyden, 1970.

Gould, R. The phases of adult life: A study in developmental psychology. *American Journal of Psychiatry*, 1972, *129*, 521–531.

Greer, M. & Rubinstein, B. *Will the real teacher please stand up?* Pacific Palisades, Calif.: Goodyear Publishing Company, 1972.

Guardo, C. J. The helping process as developmental existentialism. *Personnel and Guidance Journal*, 1975, *53*, 493–499.

Guerney, B. G., et al. A format for a new mode of psychological practice: Or how to escape a zombie. *Counseling Psychologist*, 1970, *2*, 94–104.

Havighurst, R. J. *Human development and education.* New York: Longmans, Green and Co., 1953.

Heath, D. H. *Humanizing Schools.* New York: Hayden, 1971.

Holmes, T. H., & Rahe, R. H. The social readjustment rating scale. *Journal of Psychosomatic Research*, 1967, *11*, 213–218.

Ivey, A. F., & Alschuler, A. S. An introduction to the field. *Personnel and Guidance Journal*, 1973, *51*, 591–597.

Katchadourian, H. A., and Lunde, D. T. *Fundamentals of human sexuality.* New York: Holt, Reinhart and Winston, Inc., 1972.

Kincaid, M. B. *Sex-role stereotyping: A review of research.* Arizona State University, March 1973 (mimeographed).

Kohlberg, L. Stages of moral development as a basis for moral education. In C. Beck and E. Sullivan (Eds.) *Moral Education.* Toronto, U. of Toronto Press, 1970.

Lazarus, A. A. *Behavior therapy and beyond.* New York: McGraw-Hill, 1971.

Lazarus, A. A. *Daily living: Coping with tension and anxiety.* Chicago: Instructional Dynamics, Inc., 1970 (audiotape).

Lazarus, R. S. *Psychological stress and the coping process.* New York: McGraw-Hill, 1966.

Leonard, G. *Education and ecstasy.* New York: Dell, 1968.

Levinson, D. J., et al. The psychosocial development of men in early adulthood and the mid-life transition. In D. F. Ricks, A. Thomas, and M. Roff (Eds.), *Life history research in psychopathology*, Vol. 3. Minneapolis: University of Minnesota Press, 1974, pp. 243–258.

Lidz, T. *The person: His and her development throughout the life cycle.* rev. 2nd ed. New York: Basic Books, 1976.

Lindemann, E. The symptomatology and management of acute grief. *American Journal of Psychiatry*, 1944, *101*, 141–148.

Loevinger, J. *Measuring ego development.* San Francisco: Jossey-Bass, 1970.

Masuda, M., Holmes, T. H. Magnitude estimations of social readjustment. *Journal of Psychosomatic Research*, 1967, *11*, 219–225.

Mayo, P. Sexuality. *Crisis Intervention Resource Manual.* Univ. of So. Dakota, Vermillion, So. Dak., 1973.

McCary, J. L. *Sexual Myths and Fallacies.* New York: Van Nostrand Reinhold Co., 1971.

Middleman, R. R., & Goldberg, G. The concept of structure in experiential learning. In J. W. Pfeiffer and J. E. Jones, (Eds.), *The 1972 annual handbook for group facilitators.* Iowa City: University Associates, 1972, pp. 203–210.

Moos, R. H. (Ed.) *Human adaptation.* Lexington, Mass: D. C. Heath and Co., 1976.

Morgan, L. B. Counseling for future shock. *Personnel and Guidance Journal,* 1974, *42,* 283–287.

Morrison, E. S., & Price, M. U. *Values in sexuality—A new approach to sex education.* New York: Hart Publishing Co., 1974.

Mosher, R. L., & Sprinthall, N. A. Psychological education. *Counseling Psychologist,* 1971, *2,* 3–82.

Nelson, R. C., & Bloom, J. W. *Choice awareness: An innovative guidance process.* Boston: Houghton Mifflin, 1975.

Parkes, C. M. *Bereavement: Studies of grief in adult life.* New York: International Universities Press, 1972.

Patterson, C. H. *Humanistic Education.* New York: Prentice-Hall, 1973.

Patterson, G. R., & Gullion, M. E. *Living with children.* Champaign, Ill.: Research Press, 1971.

Paykel, E. S., et al. Life events and depression: A controlled study. *Archives of General Psychiatry,* 1969, *21,* 753–760.

Paykel, E. S., et al. Scaling of life events. *Archives of General Psychiatry,* 1971, *23,* 340–347.

Pfeiffer, J. W., & Jones, J. E. *A handbook of structured experiences for human relations training,* Vols. I–IV. San Diego: University Associates Press, 1969.

Piaget, J. *The construction of reality in the child.* New York: Basic Books, 1954.

Poland, R. *Human experience.* St. Louis: Mosby, 1974.

Purves, A. C. (Ed.) *How porcupines make love: Notes on a response-centered curriculum.* Lexington, Mass.: Xerox College Publishing, 1972.

Rahe, R. H., et al. Prediction of near-future health change from subjects preceding life change. *Journal of Psychosomatic Research,* 1970, *14,* 400–401.

Raths, L., Harmin, M., & Simon, S. *Values and teaching.* Columbus, Ohio: Charles Merrill, 1966.

Satir, V. *Peoplemaking.* Palo Alto, Calif.: Science and Behavior Books, 1972.

Saulman, K. A. *Memoirs of an ex-prom queen.* New York: Bantam, 1972.

Sharp, B. B. *Learning: The rhythm of risk.* Rosemont, Ill.: Combined Motivation Education Systems, 1971.

Sheehy, G. *Passages.* New York: E. P. Dutton, 1976.

Simon, S., Howe, L., & Kirshenbaum, H. Values clarification: A handbook of practical strategies for teachers and students. New York: Hart Publishing Co., 1972.

Simon, S. *Meeting yourself halfway.* Niles, Ill.: Argus Communications, 1974.

Stevens, J. O. *Awareness: Exploring, experimenting, experiencing.* Lafayette, Calif.: Real People Press, 1971.

Stillman, I., & Baker S. *Doctor's quick weight-loss diet.* New York: Prentice-Hall, 1967.

Thoreson, C. E., & Mahoney, M. J. *Behavioral self-control.* New York: Holt, Rinehart and Winston, 1974.

Toffler, A. *Future shock.* New York: Random House, 1970.

Tryon, C., & Lilienthal, J. W. Developmental tasks: The concept and its importance. In *Fostering mental health in our schools.* Washington, D.C.: National Education Association, 1950.

Walz, G. R. Swinging into the future. *Personnel and Guidance Journal,* 1975, *53,* 712–716.

Watson, D. L. and Tharp, R. G. *Self-directed behavior: Self-modification for personal adjustment.* Belmont, Calif.: Brooks/Cole, 1972.

Weinstein, G., and Fantini, M. D. *Toward humanistic education.* New York: Praeger, 1970.

Williams, R. L., & Long, J. D. *Toward a self-managed life style.* Boston: Houghton Mifflin, 1975.

Zaccaria, J. S. Developmental tasks: Implications for the goals of guidance. *Personnel and Guidance Journal,* 1965, *44,* 373–375.

Zahorik, J. A., & Brubaker, D. L. *Toward more humanistic instruction.* Dubuque, Iowa: Brown, 1972.